THE TRINITY AND THE
RELIGIOUS EXPERIENCE OF MAN

By the same author

THE UNKNOWN CHRIST OF HINDUISM
WORSHIP AND SECULAR MAN

The Trinity and the Religious Experience of Man

Icon—Person—Mystery

RAIMUNDO PANIKKAR

ORBIS BOOKS
NEW YORK
DARTON, LONGMAN & TODD
LONDON

Darton, Longman & Todd Limited
85 Gloucester Road, London SW7 4SU

ISBN 0 232 51200 0

Orbis Books, Maryknoll, New York 10545

ISBN 0-88344-495-x

© 1973 Raimundo Panikkar

First published 1973

Printed in Great Britain by
The Anchor Press Limited and
bound by William Brendon & Son Limited,
both of Tiptree, Essex

CONTENTS

PREFACE

This study was written ten years ago in Uttarkāshi in the heart of the Himalayas in a small hut on the shore of the Ganges. The fact that my silence was broken or challenged, and certainly enriched, by Swami Abhishiktānanda, to whom *namaskāras* are here proffered, made me write down my insights in French. It was Mary Rogers, to whom thanks are here given, who kindly translated the unpublished French manuscript into English for an Indian edition. It is my own self who has revised the whole text for this present edition in another small, and almost antipodal town, this time on the shores of the Pacific Ocean. Human and physical geography have played a part in eliciting the universal character of these overcondensed pages. Any human problem today that is not put thematically over against the global human horizon is bound to remain at the surface of the problem itself without reaching the depths of humanness, touching neither the heart of the matter nor the shores of the divine. On the other hand, any human problem which remains abstract and is not concrete and lived in a real and thus limited situation is bound to remain shallow and swim in the muddy waters of sheer generalities.

It has been excruciating to re-enact an experience without being able to express it in at least five hundred pages. I need to write at that length to make myself understood, and to offer a sympathetic treatise on the history and philosophy of the conception of the Trinity throughout the ages and within the several

religious traditions of mankind. It is simply an unwarranted over-
statement to affirm that the trinitarian conception of the Ultimate, and with it of the whole of reality, is an exclusive Christian
insight or revelation.

The question begins by being a semantic problem. Nowhere does
one suffer more from what St Thomas Aquinas, precisely when
he was writing on the same mystery (*S.Th.* I, 37 :1), called the
inopia vocabulorum, the misery of terms. The appeal of silence
becomes sometimes almost overwhelming and often even obses-
sive ('deep, the abyss, calls to deep'—Ps. 42(41):7). But the
human predicament is a speaking one. Even more, the truth *lies* in
the interpretation (in both senses of the word), and we cannot renounce truth—even if every word, with exception of the ultimate Word, contains also a lie, inasmuch as it always says more
and less than what both the speaker and the hearer can grasp.

The only human way to escape the snare of single words (like
those of 'God', 'person', 'man', in our case) is also what the same
tradition used to call the *nexus mysteriorum*, the internal consist-
ency and inter-relatedness of the ultimate mysteries of the world
(*Denz.* 3016); i.e. the plausible congruency of a system of words
within an accepted world-view, so that one idea sustains the other
and one concept fits well into the space provided by another, pro-
viding a coherent and harmonious world-picture. It is precisely because of this interconnection that when the frame of reference
changes, the words also undergo a similiar process in order to convey the original insights. The text is always dependent on a
context and, if the latter varies, the text has also to change
accordingly if the original message or meaning of the text is to be
preserved. It is only over against our conception of reality, that
is our present myth (as ultimate frame of reference which we take
for granted) that our words and concepts are intelligible. It is,
thus, only by re-enacting or, let us say, by again incarnating the

traditional experiences of mankind that we may be loyal to them and, furthermore, it is only in this way that we can deepen them and continue the real tradition. Authentic tradition does not consist in handing down dead formulae or anachronistic customs, but passing on the living flame of man's memory and life. There is no *logos* without *myth* or *myth* without *logos*. In every *logos* there is a *myth*, the *myth* that the *logos* says. In every *myth* there is a *logos*, the *logos* that tells the *myth*.

Myth and logos meet in the symbol. No man can live without symbols. The symbol is the true appearance of reality; it is the form in which, in each case, reality discloses itself to our consciousness, or rather, it is that particular consciousness of reality. It is in the symbol that the real appears to us. It is not reality (which never exists naked, as it were) but its manifestation, its revelation. The symbol is not another 'thing', but the epiphany of that 'thing' which is-not without some symbol—because ultimately Being itself is the final symbol. Any real symbol encompasses and unites both the symbolised 'thing' and the consciousness of it.

All this is not a mere disquisition in defence of my own formulations regarding the Trinity. I am rather concerned with a more universal principle regarding words and sentences. The moment that words say only exactly what you mean and do not leave room for what I may also mean, the moment that they become only signs and cease to be symbols, the moment that they only signal something else and are no longer the expression, the manifestation and with it the veil itself of that 'else', in that moment they degenerate even as words. They become mere tools for transmission of coded messages, open only to those who previously possess the clue. Words may then very easily become means of oppression, tools of power in the mouths or hands of those who dictate their meaning or know the key to decipher the signs. You can neither interpret nor under-stand those signs; they are only orders or warnings for your orientation, but neither part of you nor revelations of reality. You can neither play nor pray, let alone be with those signs. You cannot truly speak those words, but only repeat them, aping those who impose such a power on you. When a word designates only what you mean and excludes my having part in shaping the meaning of the word also, it becomes barren, closes you up and frightens me, instead of allowing a flow of communication between us that would, by this very fact, fecundate each other and bring us nearer not only to one another but also to reality, to truth.

Even assuming that one particular group and not another sets the meaning of a word, how is the second group going to know that meaning if not by means of another sign and so on *ad infinitum*? Real words are not mere instruments in your hands or mine, they are part of the human, cosmic, and also divine interplay and they mean what we all agree that they mean in the very act of the dialogical interchange. Otherwise, they are no longer living words; they are dead.

It was not without a profound wisdom that condensed and often cryptic sentences, like crystallisations of many words, were in India called *sūtras*, i.e. threads, strings which in an aphoristic and seminal way try to link us with some of the great intuitions of mankind. A *sūtra* is a *suture* which stitches together not by means of an artificial surgery but by the power of things themselves, not only the many and complicated thoughts of more elaborated treatises, but also ourselves with the reality revealed and concealed in the *sūtras* themselves.

This study certainly is not a treatise nor can it be a *sūtra* because the treatise, out of which the *sūtra* should be distilled, has not yet been written. The author, however, believes that he expresses not a private opinion, but a paradigm of an experience which is bound to become more and more frequent in our time : the experience of gathering or rather concentrating in oneself more than one of the human phyla in which mankind's fundamental insights have accumulated. We want to be no longer sons of Manu or Israel or Ishmael alone, but children of Man.

The different traits here taken into account are brought together to form a tress which represents one of the deepest intuitions man has had and is still having, from different points of view and with different names : the intuition of the threefold structure of reality, of the triadic oneness existing on all levels of consciousness and of reality, of the Trinity. We are not saying that the idea of the Trinity can be reduced to the discovery of a triple dimension of Being, nor that this aspect is a mere rational discovery. We are only affirming that the Trinity is the acme of a truth that permeates all realms of being and consciousness and that this vision links us together.

In times of crisis and rapid change one of the greatest dangers and temptations consists in being not radical enough, due to the lack of patience and depth, both necessary in order to strike at the very roots of the situation. We refer to the danger of superficiality, of remaining on the surface of things and events and of being satisfied with statistics and a certain type of sociological description. The attempt of this essay is just the opposite of escaping into merely 'speculative' or 'theological' realms as a desperate refuge from everyday life or daily human problems pressing from all sides. Life in Europe, India and America has taught and shown me that there are no more *urgent* questions than the ultimately *important* issues, and that there is no more felt need and no more torturing thirst than the desire to tackle concrete human problems not only in a universal, global manner, but also in their ultimate meaning and at the level of their deepest roots. Neither from bread alone, nor from word alone does man live. Neither matter alone, nor spirit alone will do; nor can Man be without God nor

God without Man. Is not the Trinity the 'place' where bread and
word meet? Where God and Man meet? A non-trinitarian God
cannot 'mingle' and much less unite himself with Man without
destroying himself. He would have to remain aloof, isolated. No
incarnation, descent and real manifestation of any kind would be
possible. He would cease to be God if he became Man. A non-
trinitarian Man cannot jump outside his little self, cannot become
what he wants and longs for without destroying himself. He would
have to remain aloof, isolated. No divinisation, glorification, redemption of any kind would be possible. He would cease to be
Man if he became God. Man would stifle within himself just as
God would die of self-consumption if the trinitarian structure of
reality were not the case.

Seen from this perspective the problem of the Trinity is one of
the deepest problems Man can ask about himself and his God,
about Creation and Creator, and one of the most universal. It is
not only one of the (theoretically) most *important*, but also one of
the (practically) most *urgent* queries. It represents one of those
basic issues at the very root of our human situation with direct
relevance to questions like those of a more just society and a more
integrated human personality. Peace and human happiness, readi-
ness to act, goals in work and inspiration in art are not disconnected values nor are they independent of the ultimate horizon
of human existence. They depend to a great extent on how man
lives his underlying myth, how he envisions his situation and his
role in life—all of them problems directly connected with the
Trinity. The doctrine of the Trinity, in point of fact, is not there
for the sake of satisfying our curiosity about the 'immanent'
Trinity as an internal affair of the Divinity (*ad intra*), alone. It
connects the immanent mystery with the 'economic' God
(*ad extra*), in which the destiny of the whole world is at stake. It
is not mere speculation about the depths of God; it is equally an

analysis of the heights of Man. It is a 'revelation' of God inasmuch as it is a revelation of Man.

The modern devastating dilemma, for instance, between an un-
convincing traditional 'God' and a less convincing modern 'No-
God' is resolved by the trinitarian conception. The Trinity, in
fact, makes it impossible to consider God as a substance (it would
then amount to modalism or to tritheism), to consider him as a
totally 'other' (this dualism would then be unbridgeable). 'God'
is *nomen potestatis non proprietatis*, a name designing a function
of power and not an ontological attribute. Thus says an old con-
fession of Christian belief, the *Fides Damasi* (*Denz.* 71). To get
rid of the notion of an ever scrutinising and judging 'God', of
somebody who deprives man of his ultimate responsibility and
condones intolerable human situations represents a step ahead in
human maturity if, at the same time, one does not fall into the
other horn of the dilemma : that of a shortsighted atheism which
is closed to true transcendence as well as genuine immanence.
The idea of the Trinity maintains an openness in human existence,
vouches for infinite possibilities and while accepting atheistic
criticism, offers the possibility of hope and the guarantee of free-
dom. The Trinity in fact, reveals that there is life in the Godhead
as well as in Man, that God is not an idol, nor a mere idea, nor an
ideal goal of human consciousness. Yet he is neither another substance nor a separate, and thus separable, reality.

The agreement here should not be found in a common de-
nominator, which would be obtained by chopping off all that is
positive, valuable and distinctive, agreeing only in what is
irrelevant and banal. It is not found by giving up the theistic
affirmations and emasculating the atheistic convictions, but by
transcending both without negating them.

The same can be said in the field of the world religions. A
coalition in order to fight 'disbelief' or to defend 'religious values'

is not agreement but mere partisan strategy. If the religions of the
world have to agree with each other and have to serve contemporary man, they have to forget 'holy' alliances, overcome monopolis-
ing attitudes and come to grips with central and fundamental
issues regaining those levels in which understanding is possible
without compromise and uniformity. The deepening into the
trinitarian structure of religious experience and of human beliefs
may here again offer a possibility of fecundation, agreement and
collaboration not only among religions themselves, but also with
modern man at large, so often torn apart by religious subtleties
which he does not understand.

I must finish this preface with a word of true humility. The
author is convinced of all that he says. He is also convinced that all
that he says is not what he would like to say, but he does not
know how to say it better and, until a certain dialogue has taken
place, it cannot be said better. He is further convinced that what
he says is only a hypothesis, an insinuation and an invitation to
enter that path in which the divine depths and the human heights
meet, where the necessary distinctions between philosophy and
theology, matter and spirit, reason and faith, God and Man, one
religious tradition and another, are not blurred, but where they
do not become lethal separations either.

One insight may be considered central in the pages that follow :
a cosmotheandric and thus non-dualistic vision of reality. I may
sum it up in three brief paragraphs.

1. The first refers to the universality of the experience and the
reality of the so-called three persons (in the singular and in the
plural) as represented by the personal pronouns. There are languages which do not have the verb 'to be' and others which do
not possess the word 'being'. In some there is no definite distinction between nouns and verbs. No known language lacks the 'I,
Thou, He/She/It' with the respective plural forms. It is in this

ultimate and universal structure that the Trinity is reflected or, to speak theologically, because the Trinity is 'I, Thou, He/She/It, We, You, They', human experience presents this character. The Trinity appears then as the ultimate paradigm of personal relationships (and neither substantial nor verbal).

2. The second refers to the radical inter-relationship of everything in spite of the artificial separations which our minds tend to make when they lose the patience and the humility of considering the constitutive connections of all that is. In one way or another, no total excommunication is true in the sphere of the real. These relationships encompass and constitute the entire web of reality. The Trinity as pure relation epitomises the radical relativity of all that there is.

3. The third refers to the fundamental unity of reality, which should not be overshadowed by the diversity of the whole universe. The variety of beings, including the theological difference between the divine and the created or God and the world, should not overshadow the fundamental unity of reality. It is in the human experience of the person that we have a clue to this mystery of unity and diversity and it is the Trinity which offers us the ultimate model of this all-pervading constitution of reality. The person is neither monolithic oneness nor disconnected plurality. A singular isolated person is a contradiction in terms. Person implies constitutive relationship, the relationship expressed in the pronominal persons. An *I* implies a *thou*, and as long as this relation is being maintained it implies also a *he/she/it* as the place where the *I–thou* relation takes place. An *I–thou* relation implies equally a *We–you* dimension, which includes the *they* in a similar way as the *he/she/it* is included in the *I–thou*. On the other hand, the person, properly speaking does not allow for any plural, it is not quantifiable. Five persons are neither more nor less than ten persons. What we mean by those figures is only individuals, but the individual is precisely

not the person, but only an abstraction for pragmatic reasons. What we generally call a person is what presents the structure of a *thou*, the second person—if we still like to use the 'personalistic' language. This model helps us to understand better the Trinity and at the same time the mystery of the Trinity opens us up so that we may grasp better the ultimate constitution of the real.

But in order to elaborate all this and substantiate it, we would require the abovementioned 'treatise' and what we offer now here is only an invitation to participate more abundantly in the gift of Life.

> *Caritas Pater est,*
> *Gratia Filius,*
> *Communicatio Spiritus Sanctus,*
> *O beata Trinitas!*

R.P.

Santa Barbara, California
Easter, 1973

INTRODUCTION

There is in existence a certain conception of the science of religions which is drained of life, sterilised, one might say, and constantly liable to stop short at the level of phenomenon—a conception that consists in viewing these religions simply and solely as historical data judged with reference to their cultural *manifestations*. The result of this is to identify in practice a given religion with its *sociological form*, i.e. with the 'clothing' it assumes in history in a particular milieu. When one proceeds to compare this religion, viewed from outside, with the faith and deep values of another religion or world-view, this latter lived from within, the result can only be negative. It is obvious that a methodological error of this sort at once invalidates any conclusion one might claim to draw from it. Penetration 'within', then, is highly essential if there is to be an authentic science of religions and an adequate discernment of spirits.

Now, on the other hand, it would appear that if one lives one's own religion with faith and from within, one is *ipso facto* obliged to refuse or contradict other religions. Is it possible, while adhering sincerely and convincedly to one religion, to show one's self unprejudiced and just towards another? Does contemporary dialogue, in order to be sincere, require an abandonment or at least a methodological 'epoché', a putting into brackets or keeping in suspense, of one's own convictions? Where this question is answered in the affirmative, the science of religions, in order to preserve impartiality, has chosen to remain outside any religious commitment. Now the consequence of this apparent neutrality is that one ends up with a fundamental misconstruing of the very core of religious belief. This is because the belief of the believer— and not only the objectifiable doctrine—belongs essentially to the religious phenomenon. And this belief cannot be understood except by a certain kind of participation.

Phenomenology permits us to compare religious phenomena but it amounts at the most to a comparison of their structures or doctrines. It cannot take the place of a philosophy or theology of religions which alone possesses the requisite vitality for an understanding in depth between the intuitions of one religion and those of another such as may lead to a mutual fecundation.

In the present study we shall aim at acquiring some reciprocal understanding of the real 'within-ness' of religions from a point of view which is originally christian but by no means exclusive, in the hope that a fresh point of view may enter the dialogue. Let me, therefore, embark on a sincere soliloquy that may lead on to dialogue, and play my part, all the time conscious of the fact, however, that even the most perfect melody is a poor substitute for the grand symphony which we await and for which we long.

Every christian who lives his faith, and has a personal experience of the mystery of Christ, will refuse to reduce christian reality to the compass of his own individual experience, however precious and essential that experience may appear to him to be. Even less will he reduce it to any particular expression of christianity manifested at some one particular period of history. Seen and lived from within, reality unveiled by faith is something far deeper than all individual and sociological forms that it may assume, something far richer than any translation of it in cultural, philosophical, theological or even religious terms that man may use to explain it. The same is valid, of course, for any other traditional creed.

By a remarkable paradox the more one lives a faith subjectively, that is, the more one assimilates and makes it one's own, the more conscious and respectful one becomes of its objectivity, the more one discovers a remnant which cannot be assimilated. In a word, there is a positive and strict correlation between all authentic subjectivity and all true objectivity. Modernist 'subjectivity' is erroneous when it eliminates objectivity; but even more erroneous is juridical objectivity—and legalism—when it stifles all true subjectivity.

This distinction between *essence* and *form* is vital nowadays as regards all religious awareness and notably as regards christianity. Its catholicity, in fact its claim to universality, renders absolutely necessary its dissociation from every sort of cultural garment—which is for christianity particularly difficult by reason of the ponderous greek heritage that impels it in a well-nigh irresistible fashion to regard the *morphé*, the 'form', of a thing as its essence. In a theology or philosophy where *nāmarūpa*, name and form, is in one way or another the expression of the simple appearance of things, a change of forms would be far simpler. Furthermore, for a culture which, despite the progressive secularisation of the concept of *logos* to the point of its being reduced to an equivalent of reason, has still not completely forgotten its divine origin and thus still retains atavistic traces of the respect owed to the divinity, all change of *logoi* becomes highly suspect. However, that is not the sole possible way of accepting and recognising the one who said that 'The Father is greater than I' and refused outright the title of 'good', the one who was despoiled and crushed, the one who told us 'If a grain does not fall into the ground and die . . .' Let us go further: christian 'stripping' should be complete. The faith of the enlightened christian must strip itself of the 'christian religion' as it actually exists and free itself for a fecundation that will affect all religions both ancient and modern. From the sociological and external point of view christianity is only one religion among others. One can therefore compare christianity with these other religions because it is one among the rest. From a sociological and even 'scientific' point of view one cannot any longer consider christianity as the whole of 'religion' as if the rest were not religions or were false religions. On the contrary the faith that I still desire to call christian, though others may prefer to call it simply human, leads to the *plenitude* and hence to the *conversion* of all religion, even though up to date it has only succeeded, from a judaic substructure in converting to a greater or lesser extent helleno-latin-gothic-celtic 'paganism'. This same faith is at the present time engaged in the process of converting modern secularism.

Christian faith, however, lives within time and in the hearts of men. It requires, therefore, to be 'incarnated' in a historical form; but what we call christianity is only one form among other possible ones of living and realising the christian faith. In point of fact the dominant form in which christianity is at present lived is incontestably that which it has adopted little by little in the course of the history of the western world. We have no right at all, however, to identify this particular sociological form with christian faith itself. To do so would involve on the one hand a particularism incompatible with catholicity and in the other an ana-chronistic theological colonialism that is absolutely unacceptable.

Just as it is not possible to wish to stop the evolving process of history at a given point, so it is even less possible to start all over again, *ab ovo*, from scratch. The actual forms or expressions of christianity, even its theological ones, may become outworn but nevertheless we have no power to jettison them outright or replace them by others which may appear more appropriate at this particular juncture, without taking into account the claims of tradition, that is to say, the historical link between past and future. To act thus would be not only barbaric but false and ultimately impossible. Continuity must not be ruptured; development must occur harmoniously, enrichment progressively and transformation in accordance with nature. This process must involve a *sui generis* assimilation of new values or it may come about through the coming to light of hitherto neglected aspects—in a word, by a vital process of growth in which substitution happens less by rejection than by assumption.

Such a process is called for firstly and unceasingly in response to the demand of truth, but doubly so today with an insistence and ever-growing urgency, for it constitutes the very *kairós* the moment of destiny, of our age, a *kairós* that is precipitated both by this modern world which challenges traditional religions with its own values that it refuses to call religious, and also by the mutual encounter of those world religions with changes, all of them at their deepest levels.

In these pages I wish to suggest certain lines of thought capable, I consider, of aiding this deepening and universalisation of faith so necessary in our day and age. In undertaking this one desires above all to follow a method of universal religious validity and not adopt a sectarian viewpoint for the benefit of one group. By collaborating towards the *universalisation* of christianity, towards the actualisation in fact of its catholicity, one is contributing to the development of all religions towards unity. There is no question here of criticising certain religious forms that may be good in themselves and even indispensible to man at certain stages of the development of his consciousness and of the march of history; rather I am attempting to trace out the guidelines which faith seems challenged to follow in order to become deeper and more universal. If I take christianity as my point of departure it is not out of partiality or sectarianism but because it is necessary to start somewhere and I believe that christianity is especially called to 'suffer' this purifying transformation. In fact it seems to be christians who today more than others feel vividly the urgency of such an 'opening'.

I emphasise once and for all that I *believe* this interpretation to be authentically *orthodox*—i.e. which gives to God a truly right (*orthos*) honour and glory (*doxa*)—and to be thus fully ecclesial. I am mot unaware, on the other hand, of the difficulties and danger of using expressions that are sometimes not very common ones. I hope that they will be interpreted always in accordance with the whole continuing tradition of the church.

After studying the three most characteristic forms of spirituality that are to be found as a human invariant in the majority of religions, we shall venture a consideration of the *theological* problem of the Trinity, that mystery which out of a kind of reverential awe has been virtually allowed to *atrophy* in a great part of christianity. In the third part of our study we shall embark on an outline of what I would call, following an ancient tradition, *theandrism*, i.e. the fundamental attitude through which we are enabled to understand and share the basic insights of most of the religions of the world. This procedure attempts to open up an avenue to which a merely intellectual exchange of ideas or an 'epoché' of faith could never grant access.

For seven years I have hesitated to publish these notes as they are; I wondered whether I should not develop them into a sizable volume, with all the scientific and theological documentation required for a fuller exposition and justification of my views. However, at the risk of offering here only a preliminary sketch I have finally decided to share with others this schema for correction and development—and also to be experienced and lived.

During this period I have compelled myself to clarify my thought as much as possible by working over again my original formulations of it which, although at times more striking than my current ones, might have been misunderstood. I have discovered by so doing that a piece of writing is not only, as I had thought, a gesture and an expression of an attitude but also a communication. People frequently tell me that it is not so much a question of expressing myself as of conveying my thoughts to the reader. So, then, let me welcome the go-between, communicating rôle of the idea and immerse myself in life . . .

Let me make one last observation. If I have decided to publish this script as it is, without the numerous notes that might lend it weight and authority, it is specifically because it is far more a meditation than an erudite study, far more a mystical and 'praying' theology than an analytical and cogitative philosophy (though we must refrain from pressing the distinction to the point of dichotomy.) It is in Faith, Hope and Love that the following pages have been lived. I refer to the past, for of my present life I cannot speak . . .

I. FORMS OF SPIRITUALITY

Let us start by defining any given spirituality, pragmatically and even phenomenologically, as being one typical way of handling the human condition. Next let us put this in more religious terms by saying that it represents man's basic attitude *vis-à-vis* his ultimate end. In either case I think that the following classification will help us to see our way through the dense forest of world religions. One of the features that differentiates a spirituality from an established religion is that the former is far more flexible, for it is disconnected from the mass of rites, structures, etc., that are indispensable to all religions. One religion, in fact, may include several spiritualities, because spirituality is not directly bound up with any dogma or institution. It is rather an attitude of mind which one may ascribe to different religions.

It would be possible to put forward almost innumerable classifications but I consider that the one I am adopting is acceptable from several points of view. It belongs in fact to more than one religious tradition and offers us a trinitarian formulation which is applicable to many of them. Furthermore this schema is authenticated anthropologically inasmuch as it is in correspondence with the actual constitution of man as man. Finally it does not proceed from an *a priori* construction but emerges from an empirical assessment of the situation.

My exposition of the theme will clarify these remarks; but in order to take our bearings without delay we may define three forms of spirituality, *viz.* of action, love and knowledge, or, to put it in other terms, spiritualities centred around iconolatry, personalism and mysticism.

A man may seek to handle his condition of 'humanness' by adopting an image, an idol, an icon, which is at one and the same time outside (attracting), inside (inspiring), and above (directing). It is this which gives to the life of man, to his moral character, his thought and aspirations, a proper orientation and stimulus for action.

One may also attempt to establish another kind of relationship with what I would call (to attempt some name) the Absolute. One may consider it as the mystery hidden in the very depth of the human soul which can only be unveiled and galvanised by love, by an intimate personal relationship, by dialogue. In this case God is the essential pole which not only orientates, so to speak, the human personality, but is also its constitutive element, for one cannot live or 'be' without love and one cannot love without that third dimension of verticality which is only realised in the discovery of the divine person.

The third form of spirituality stresses the demands of thought and the exigencies of reason, or rather of the intellect or intuition; it rejects a God constructed more or less according to its own measure and its own needs and seeks to penetrate to the ultimate analysis of being and to find there a vision which enables man to live while accepting to the full his own humanness.

Of course the examples given are merely illustrative; this does not purport to be a historical study or an account of an evolutionary process in time. I would prefer to call it an essay in *kairological* dialectic. It is in order to take the temperature of our times that these incursions into the past are here attempted.

ICONOLATRY—KARMAMĀRGA

To explain what I mean, the term that springs to mind is idolatry. I might well choose this word out of a desire to defend the good name of many so-called idolaters against the caricature drawn by others of what is in fact one of the most important expressions of adoration and religiousness. Yet, the fact that one cannot deny the misuse of it and the degradations that still do derive from this primordial human urge, together with the recognition of the bad taste left by this word in the minds of many, causes me to abandon its use and coin the term *iconolatry* to indicate this primary and primordial attitude of man in front of the divinity or the mystery (whether *fascinans, tremendum* or any other sort).

The question as to whether God has made man in his own image and likeness is open to discussion; but that man has given himself, or has had implanted within him, an idea of the divinity as being in his own image and likeness is indubitable. Otherwise it would be impossible for him to come into contact with the divine either by word or concept. We will try to describe this attitude by taking a somewhat paradoxical example, that of Israel who has too frequently been cited as being the reverse of iconolatrous.

No one can deny that throughout her long history ancient Isreal was as a people seriously tempted by idolatry. Not only did Israel fall from time to time into what her Law considered the supreme sin, that sin which Jahweh by the mouth of his prophets was compelled constantly to combat, but, looked at closely as regards her whole spirituality, her idea of God and her whole worship, the religion of Israel belonged to the category of idolatrous or rather iconolatrous religions. Idolatry constitutes a sort of *leit motif* running through the books of the Old Testament. This was in fact the reason why the worship of *false* idols was for Israel both the greatest sin and the greatest temptation. Grass is no source of temptation to the lion while the cow feels no yearning for meat!

There is undoubtedly a fundamental distinction in the eyes of Israel between the Jewish type of idolatry and the idolatry of her neighbouring peoples. The idol of Israel was certainly not an object made by hand or created by thought, and invention or discovery of man; it was Jahweh, the living and true God, the One who had revealed himself to Israel and made a pact with her, who was Israel's own special idol. Israel's idol was one symbolising the Truth and not merely a true idol. Yet the fact that Jahweh was Truth made no difference to the character of the relationship that he had with his people. A morphological study of the religion of Israel and the religions of the surrounding canaanite peoples would reveal at once that, for their faithful, Jahweh and the gods of the *goïm* are situated on the same level. It is this very fact that explains the unrelieved struggle described in the Bible between Jahweh Sabaoth and his 'rivals', the other gods, the gods of the nations. In order to maintain his position as the one and only idol of Israel, Jahweh was obliged to fight these others, and owed it to himself to do so with the vigour of which we all know. The other gods were false gods precisely because they were false idols. We need not discuss their power or their relative and limited sovereignty; we may simply state that for Israel they do not constitute the idol which corresponds to the biblical theophany of God. Rivalry does not come into existence except between realities of the same order. Reverting to the absurdity mentioned above we might say that competition is not possible between cows of the pasture and fish of the sea.

It is not part of our present thesis to explain in detail how the worship of Jahweh, and that of the other gods were morphologically equivalent. It is sufficient to read the Bible and the accounts in history of, for example, the gods of Moab and Assyria. In any case the Israelites were experienced idolaters; they had no need of a mentor to teach them to fashion and pay homage to idols. As early on as their desert experience it only needed forty days without their leader Moses for them to substitute a golden calf in the place of their living but invisible idol Jahweh. Everything is in the same vein. Jahweh *exists* in the Ark and dwells in his Temple just as Ashtaroth, Baal and Dagon do in theirs. The Hebrews speak of, behave towards, and pray to Jahweh in the very same manner as the canaanites speak of, behave towards, and pray to their gods. They worship him just as an idol is worshipped the essence of iconolatry not consisting, as we shall explain in a moment, in the material character of the idol but in the act of attributing to God creaturely qualities and attributes which are refined to a greater or lesser extent and can be ascertained by various procedures.

We should add at once that iconolatry represents a normal dimension of the religious life of man and even of the manifestation of God to man. Do not the Fathers of the Church teach us that the Lord in his condescension always adapted himself to the needs and possibilities of man, only manifesting himself in correspondence with man's ability to receive his message and put it into practice? This evolution of awareness is similarly observable in the individual. Religion, in fact, could not come into being without at least some traces of iconolatry, just as without some traces of impurity in the physical elements no chemical reaction would be set in motion. No 'chemically pure' religion is conceivable except in the case of an artificially 'pure' individual, stages removed from man as he is, *in statu nascendi*, in a state of becoming.

Is it, then, in actual fact iconolatry itself that is attacked by the prophets, or rather false idolatry, that of the rivals of Jahweh? The corner-stone of the Torah is in actuality emphasising the exclusive nature of God's revelation to the chosen people. 'Hear, O Israel . . . *Thou* shalt have no other God than *Me*' (Deut. 5 : 1 ; 6 : 14). This is a directive for Israel, not applying to other peoples. It is a manifestation of the God of Israel who is over and above other gods. For Israel Jahweh is the Supreme Lord (cf. Deut. 6 : 4), and therefore he is also a 'jealous God' (Deut. 5 : 9; 6 : 15). Although under the influence of the later prophets the israelite conception of God will doubtless be 'purified', yet never, generally speaking at least, will it lose completely its iconolatrous character.

Mediterranean christianity, which inherited the jewish prophets, has always exhibited a sort of instinctive horror of idolatry—and this has not failed to cause tragic misunderstandings when christianity has come in contact with the religions of Africa and Asia. Nevertheless, her own most widespread religious attitude seems to lend considerable support to our thesis. People continue to assert loudly that idolatry is the most degraded and degenerate form of religion and yet scarcely have they, in accordance with this view, snatched the wooden or stone idol brusquely from its stand or niche than they hasten to install in its place, as the object of similiar worship, the God-icon of Israel or even the image that they have made for themselves of God revealed in Christ. 'We already have Kṛṣṇa', rejoin hindus. Why do you want us to substitute your Christ in his place? One idol is as good as another.'

We are not interested here, let me repeat, in either defending or condemning iconolatry. We are only maintaining that the spirituality of Israel, based on the conception of a God who speaks, punishes, pardons, is jealous, ordains laws, can be offended and also appeased, who commands, promises and concludes pacts with men, etc., belongs phenomenologically to the category of iconolatry, for such behaviour appertains to all icons. The sole difference—a fundamental one, we repeat, for the sons of Abraham—is that in one instance there is involved the living and true God, invisible, creator of the world, and in the other instances an identification, often a hasty and immature one, between concrete idol and God supreme, not always sufficiently qualified.

After all, in what does iconolatry consist if not in the projection of God under some *form*, his objectivation, his personification *in* an *object* which may be mental or material, visible or invisible, but always reducible to our human 'representation'? Iconolatry is in fact religious cosmo-anthropomorphism, the attribution to God of 'creaturely' forms, whether supra-human or sub-human. It makes no ultimate difference whether these forms are gross or subtle, or even whether the iconolater is conscious or not of the inner religious attitude that is his and, as is generally the case, recognises that the iconolatrous *sign* is provisional and must yield to the underlying reality (the *res*) when the time comes. In the final analysis the icon stands for the homogeneity which subsists between God and his creature; and it is this very homogeneity, which is the condition of religion of the *re-ligatio* that 'binds together' God and Man so that they are not totally separate and heterogeneous realities. If God were *totally* other, there would be no place for love or for knowledge, or for prayer and worship, no place, indeed, for Himself-as-Other. Man spends himself for his idol, submits himself to his idol, is devoted and abandoned to his idol, because his destiny is closely linked with that of his idol. The idol is neither impassible nor inaccessible; it is implicated itself in the human adventure. There is mutuality between idol and worshipper. A man loves his idol-god because this god has become for him stone, wood, flesh. Who could spend

himself for the pure Transcendent (cf. *Gītā* XII. 5)? The pure
Transcendent, even by definition, does not concern us, being impassible, immovable, aloof from the human whirlpool. Jahweh
who suffered for Israel was the true idol; his honour was involved
with that of his people. Out of love for Israel he manifested himself to her as her idol in this particular historical period in the
evolution of religious consciousness in the human race. If cows
possessed a knowledge of God, how would they conceive him if
not in the form of a cow? A God who lacked any relationship of
form with them could not possibly be the God. Iconoclasm, thus,
is a sin against the very first commandment.

Here let us clarify our thesis further. There are two things,
idolatry and iconolatry. Idolatry, understood as the transference
to a creature of the adoration due to God alone, i.e. an adoration
which stops short at the object, without going beyond it in an on-
going movement towards the Creator, the Transcendent, is
without doubt the gravest of sins. But iconolatry which starts by
adoring some object upon which has descended the glory of the
Lord, and takes this object as a point of departure for a slow and
arduous ascent towards God, cannot be condemned and rejected
so easily. Furthermore, there exists within all idolatry a more or
less latent icon-experience, that is to say, an experience of an
iconological sort which is an essential dimension in all truly
human spirituality. This experience that God is of the likeness
(*eikōn*) of man, that God is at the image (*eidōlón*) of man, that
there is an ontological link between the two needs to be
cultivated.

To underline a parallelism to which we shall revert later we
may now introduce the concepts of *karma, bhakti,* and *jñāna*
(action, love and knowledge), borrowed from the religions of
India, as ways of spirituality. *Karma-mārga,* the way of sacred
action i.e. ritual action leading to salvation, the fulfilment of

duty, realisation of one's *dharma*, obedience to the law, the keeping of the commandments and so on, all depend upon this first spiritual dimension. If there were no God-icon to command and issue edicts, none of this would make sense. A 'philosophic' God, pure Principle, Immovable Mover, etc., cannot be the foundation of any living religion.

There is a question here of coming to an agreement *upon* words, to which we are certainly prompted by human wisdom; but we must also be in agreement *with* words, in which consists theological wisdom, i.e. we must respect them and not manipulate them in an arbitrary fashion. Now the word idol was introduced to designate a material object made by man's hand (generally) and adored as God. The idol is thus of human workmanship and is as such inferior to man, so to worship it is the worst of sins (Isaiah 44 :9 ff). We would like, however, to make two observations, the one on behalf of a great number of idolaters, and the other arising from a more general consideration.

Given this definition of idolatry as the adoration of a creature instead of the Creator, can we be so certain that the so-called idolaters always make this transference and this confusion? Is it not the same as in polytheism which only appears as such to the one who is not a polytheist? Does not the falsity in idolatry reside, not in the existential act of adoration itself, but in the undertsanding that the faithful may have of this adoration? Idolatry is not false *qua latria* (worship) but it is false *qua* objectification of this adoration. All *latria* presupposes an idol, icon, image; but is 'idolisation' worse than 'idealisation' or objectification? Moreover, are not most of the revered idols believed to have been found or originated in some mysterious ways so that they cannot be said to express just human craftsmanship? If the idol is a true image of the divinity—if one does not lose sight of the iconological character of the idol—idolatry has a place in every true religion. Idolatry only becomes erroneous when the idol is severed from its iconological connection with the divinity. Might not Israel, then, be said to be the champion of true idolatry as against false? False idols are non-existent because there is only one God (cf. the background of 1 Cor. 8:4 ff).

Thus we come to our second observation. No one can jump over his own shadow. Iconolatry is one of the basic forms of human religious consciousness. Even in the judaeo-christian context, and more so in the semitic and mediterranean religious world, the iconological and thus idolatrous dimension of the Divinity occupies the foreground. Man is the image of God, the world a divine 'vestige' and the presense of the absolute is always that of incarnation. How readily intelligible, then, is man's tendency towards adoring this divine icon under the form of one idol or another. It is quite in line with all this that meat sacrificed in the temples was called *eidōlóthyton* (sacrificed to an idol) by jews and christians, while those who offered it called it *hieróthyton* (slain as sacred or slain in sacrifice, *thoton* meaning 'sacrificed' and, thence, 'slain').

The icon does not need to be iconographically represented. On the contrary, any iconomorphic spirituality will tend to eliminate all those types of icons which do not fit its main iconological pattern : Israel will not allow 'idols'; Islam will not permit pictures : tribal religions will not care much about 'ideas' on the divine (theo*logies*); etc. The fundamental attitude however, of an iconolatric spirituality is the cultic *act* of adoration of an 'image' of God, believed to represent each time the true God. It is this action which allows us to call this spirituality *karmamārga* or the way of action in order to reach 'salvation', i.e. the end and fulfilment of man in whatever way it is interpreted.

The history of religions discloses other basic religious attitudes that are not centred upon the conception of a God-Icon. We shall refer to them later on in our study. Looking at the subject from this new perspective, one discerns a kinship between true and false idolatry that may well astonish the monotheism of jews, christians and muslims alike. It is at this point that the conception of the Trinity offers a possibility of going beyond, without denying outright, the spirituality of the icon, image or idol.

PERSONALISM—BHAKTIMĀRGA

Ancient Israel bequested to christianity, along with her scriptures, her iconological conception of God. No doubt this conception was purified and transformed both by reflection on the New Testament and by the progressive development of man's consciousness, as is shown by the later development of judaism. However it is still very much the ancient Old Testament concept of Jahweh, the God-Idol of Israel which forms the basis of the christian concept of God. Furthermore the basic material of the official prayer of the Church continues to be based on the same book of Psalms, prayed and chanted in the Temple of Jerusalem, in spite of it containing certain religious sentiments and attitudes very distant from the spirit of the Gospel.

We have, of course, no right to reduce to oversimplified outlines the complex evolution of the concept of God within christianity; nor is it permissible to reduce the picture to some few rather negative indications. If, however, we permit ourselves to mark out here, with a certain boldness perhaps, a few lines of development our aim, above all else, is to bring out the possibility of a complementary contribution which would overstep the historical boundaries of christianity as at present constituted— without wishing in any way to disparage the incomparable western contribution to the comprehension of the faith.

It is clear that the concept of God in the Gospel, especially in St John, is far removed from that of Jahweh in the jewish tradition. Whatever were the historical reasons for which Jesus was condemned, it was not for calling himself divine—this idea of the divinisation of man was neither so new nor so scandalous—but for proclaiming himself the Son of God (in the trinitarian, as it was later called, meaning of the phrase), *viz.*, begotten by God, equal to Him, coming from Him; in other words, for having dared to present himself to the people of Jahweh like the divine icon itself, which commands man's obedience and adoration and which man must needs follow, even consume. The crime of Jesus in the eyes of the jews, at least according to the christians of the first generations, was that he dared to oust Jahweh, the icon of Israel and himself occupy his place. If the 'people of God' had refused to adore 'other gods' they must certainly cast out from their midst even more vigorously one who presumed to assert that the Messiah was not a king in the 'line' of David but the true icon of the Divinity, the perfect image of Jahweh, begotten directly by Him. Jahweh can have no 'Image' because he is Himself the Idol. It is impossible to make images of God on earth because there are no archetypes in heaven to which they may correspond. Only the Trinity can rescue iconolatry. It is significant, we may note, that often the early Fathers regarded the theophanies of the Old Testament as manifestations of the Word.

However, the trinitarian scandal, which according to the theology of the first centuries cost Jesus his life, became blurred with time in some at least of christian consciousnesses. Almost imperceptibly they let themselves slip again into the legalism that Paul had denounced with such vigour. From the doctrinal point of view, the progress of a speculative kind in the approach to the trinitarian mystery was perhaps sufficiently accompanied by corresponding progress in the mystical penetration of this mystery and still less in its influence on the life and prayer of the christian. East and West were divided in this issue; while for many, the Trinity became practically a triple idol, for others it progressively yielded its place even in prayer to a so-called 'divine nature' whose mystery one was tempted to relegate to an ineffable beyond the Trinity itself—because man had reduced the Trinity to one or three images, and it is always possible to go beyond an image. For a great number of christians the Trinity became simply a highly abstract notion and for them God remained the God of Abraham, Isaac and Jacob, the great Idol whom it behoves us to worship, to appease, to please and to obey. He was, to be sure called Father but his characteristics had altered very little. He was still the Judge, Creator, Preserver, Revealer, in fact, the Other. There was, besides, a very good and real excuse for this, *viz.*, the simple recognition of the qualities of the Divine in the person of Jesus. The monolithic monotheism of orthodox judaism was revived in a certain mode of living out christianity. For many Jesus became simply the God of the christians, and this indeed is exactly the impression which is conveyed to the hindu, for example, by the occasional preaching of the Gospel that he may hear. Christians are for him those people who worship God under the name and form of Jesus.

This development leads to a parallel and complementary development in christian consciousness, resulting in what we may call in our day *personalism*. Ancient cosmo-anthropomorphism is now transformed and religious life is now founded, it is claimed, on the concept of *person*. Henceforward it is our personal relationships with God that are important because only they, it is affirmed, constitute real religion. Is not religion fundamentally a dialogue between persons? In this way certain alert sages of all ages have viewed personalism as the distinguishing feature of adult religion and it is in this direction that they desire to orient the religious evolution of humanity and, for a start, the training of christian awareness.

In religious personalism, obedience, for example, is no longer, as in iconolatry, unconditional submission but the acknowledgement of God's right to command. Love is no longer the outburst of spontaneous affection or unconscious ecstasy but a mutual giving. Worship is no longer annihilation of the self before the Absolute but the voluntary affirmation of his sovereignity. Sin is no longer cosmic transgression but a refusal to love, and so on.

Predestination, so-called, and the associate notion of divine providence are striking examples of this same trend. God foresees, God predestinates because He is someone who loves, judges, pardons, punishes, rewards—in short, does everything a person does. Remove the imperfections of the created being, cause what remains to proceed by stages upwards along the path of eminence and you will find the divine person at the end of the process. We call God a personal being *because* we ourselves are persons. We consider God a Being because we ourselves are beings. If we desire to *ascend* to God we can only begin with creatures, i.e. with ourselves. Man's *via ascensionis* to God, in his capacity as man, cannot but meet the Person. But there is also a *via descensionis* (from God to man) which is not necessarily the same path in reverse. It was by another path that the Magi returned to their homes.

However that may be, christianity has been progressively more identified with personalism, and it has been concluded that christian faith cannot take root where the concept and the experience of what is meant by a person are either unknown or insufficiently developed, since it is impossible, so it is claimed, to enter into a filial relationship with God when he has not been discovered as *person*.

As in the case of iconolatry we have no intention of impugning personalism. We want simply to guard against drawing from it exclusive conclusions or hasty extrapolations. Religious personalism is after all nothing other than a form of spirituality. Personalism and iconolatry are, in their differing degrees, inherent dimensions in every religion, corresponding to different phases of its evolution. Personalism, however, has no more right than iconolatry to identify itself with religion, since it is incapable by itself of exhausting the variety and richness of the experience of the Absolute. In so far as it claims to do so it denies its religious value and becomes irremediably false.

The way of devotion and love, *bhakti-mārga*, is the normal blossoming of the personalist dimension of spirituality. The gift of oneself to the Lord, love of God, necessarily demands a meeting of persons, a mutual acceptance and a communication between persons. The love of God cannot be inferior to human love, which it would be if the 'Beloved' could neither respond to nor love us with the intensity and purity that characterises human love. Love of God is bound to vanish if there is no dialogue, no tension, no movement towards union. 'I do not desire to cease to be,' says the *bhakta*, 'not from fear of losing myself but because love would then cease, because I then could no longer love. I do not want union but love. And it is not for *myself* that I desire love but for him What would happen if he could not love me? There are difficulties no doubt when one attempts to understand, when one tries to probe with the intelligence the mystery of love. There is someone who loves me and to whose love, though badly, I impel myself to respond with my own love, in the hope of being able to embrace him one day—a day that will know no end. If then to avoid the danger of a theoretical dualism I am forced to vanish in his arms, not only is love destroyed but the true life of the Absolute also. God can only be a person.' This concludes the *bhakta*.

If the desire for *incarnation* characterises our first dimension of spirituality and if its temptation is false idolatry, the thirst for *immanence* is the driving force behind personalism and its great temptation is anthropomorphism. Union with God does in fact find its most perfect expression in the community of love and even more so in personal communion. God is an 'I' who calls me and names me 'thou', and in calling me gives me my being and my love, i.e. my very capacity to respond to him.

However, in one whole part of the religious and spiritual tradition of humanity we find an experience of the Absolute that takes quite a different form from that proposed by personalism. The Upaniṣads for example, testify to a conception and an experience of Supreme Reality which fit poorly into the framework of a 'personalist' spirituality. This experience refuses to be reduced to the outpourings of love of the *bhakta*. Is there not in fact in all love an egoistic streak which, in the very act, in the very bosom of love, brings about the death of that same love? Love demands the renouncement of self, but when this renunciation is total, has not the object of love disappeared and has not love itself vanished in this disappearance? Does not the same thing operate with love as with *ahiṁsa*—the principle of non-violence—which, carried to its final consequences, represents the most total annihilation and denies and contradicts the principles that inspired it? To avoid killing anything one delivers oneself to death and in dying one carries the others into death. By refusing to renounce love, which fusion with the Beloved would cause to disappear, one kills love itself, for in order to be capable of continuing reciprocal love one must at all costs maintain separation and distance, which are the indispensable conditions for mutual love; but, on the other hand, it is this same love, and not only knowledge which leads to an identification, that seems to destroy the reciprocity. Thus it would seem that there remains still a place for a final step.

ADVAITA—JÑĀNAMĀRGA

The Book of the Acts and the Pauline Epistles testify to us of the deep crisis of universalism through which the Church passed in the second decade of her history. Can we truly say that even after twenty centuries the Church has entirely surmounted this initial crisis of catholicity? Perhaps we should recognise that the tension that was in evidence from the beginning forms part of the very existence of the pilgrim Church. In that day the direct appeal of the 'gentiles' to Christ was most certainly a cause of upset to the very 'pillars' of the Church, as the Council of Jerusalem records. But is not twentieth-century christianity also more or less disoriented by this appeal for universalism that is now directed towards the Church from all sides? Can we truthfully say that the Church has gone beyond the stage of the first Council or actually applied its decisions in their spirit and in all their implications? Has not christianity remained morphologically a semitic religion? The strongest proof of this is the anti-semitism that the Church tolerated, more or less, in the past, even if nowadays she feels morally bound to condemn it. One does not attack with vehemence something that does not stir one in the deepest part of one's being. The Church has never cut the umbilical cord which tied it to the Synagogue and this is right and proper; but may it not be due to this basic existential relationship that many less essential cultural elements have crept in? Has the christian conception of the Absolute passed beyond the iconolatrous stage inherited from Israel, an iconology merely purified and corrected by the personalism to which the evolution of the western world has given rise?

Let us be clear here. We are by no means seeking to minimise the privilege of the chosen people nor to disparage the special position in the divine economy which they held. Still less would

we wish to imply even a semblance of disrespect for the position
of the Old Testament. It was without doubt Israel's election at a
precisely determined moment of the historical and religious
evolution of humanity that constituted her unique glory. To the
same extent the grandeur of her religion, and of the covenant
which is its corner-stone, lies in the transcendence of both *vis-à-
vis* the world-order of which they were a part. The vocation of
Israel, as later judaism was to affirm, is to bear a burden for the
whole of humanity without debarring any man who might desire
to help her bear it.

On the other hand, however, is it not this attachment, even
limitation in practice, to a semitic socio-cultural context—or more
generally to a mediterramean one—that underlies the serious intellectual tension which exists today between the scientific men-
tality of the modern world and the believing attitude presented
by the Church? Is this not also at the very root of the tragic mis-
understanding between christian faith and the various world
religions that are still very much alive, and often lived with
intensity?

Let us recall first of all, though without undue emphasis, a
basic problem, that of *relativity*—not the relativism—of the concept of God. God is only God for the creature and with reference
to it. God is not 'God' for himself. The idea of worship is inherent within the concept of God. It would be an absurdity to say
that God can worship himself. It is the *incarnate* Son alone who
calls his Father God, and in the great theophanies of the Old
Testament Jahweh always reveals himself as the God *of* those to
whom he is manifesting himself. He never says 'I am *my* God!'
but 'I am *your* God'. God is *our* God. Without us and apart
from our relation to him God would not be 'God'. God is not
God by himself; he is so only for and hence *through* the creature.

Similarly we should not forget the historic and linguistic

origin of the word *God*. Christianity received it from the indo-european languages and religions : *deva, théos, zéus, deus, gup̄*. Far from being originally a designation of the Absolute or a meta-physical expression of the *One*, it was generally employed in the plural, in just the same way in fact as the corresponding Semitic *elohim*. The singular was usually only used to indicate the victory or supremacy of one of the *gods* over the rest or to specify the particular god of a given people or country, or the god who ruled over a particular aspect of the cosmos (rain, fire, thunder etc.).

Even the christian concept of God cannot fail to be affected by the historical horizon from which it emerged. It refers, no doubt, to the experience of the Absolute; but it also refers to the experi-ence of a theophany (Jahweh) and an epiphany (Jesus) such as occurred at a fixed time and place, was thought of and understood in a particular mental and sociological context and expressed in a given language or family of languages. Pascal was right in ob-serving that the God of the philosophers was not the God of Abraham, Isaac and Jacob. What wonder, then, that other 'philosophers' and, more especially, other sages find difficulty in identifying the Absolute of which they have experience with the God of the Patriarchs and of the judaeo-islamic-christian credo?

A concept of the Divinity which is enclosed in the traditional cultural set-up of the mediterranean world is at once fraught with enormous difficulties. One may mention right away certain metaphysical problems that unrelentingly haunt thinkers and theologians, e.g. the existence of evil and suffering, the difficulty if not impossibility of a reconciliation between human liberty and divine will, even the concept of 'person' and so on . . .

Our own times are very sensitive to the difficulties that confront the personalist conception of God. If God is a person he corres-ponds very poorly to man's own ideal of a person. Does he not show up too often as a father who is indifferent to evil and who seems to rejoice in the suffering of his children? As the price of sin he demands the blood of his Son, whom he sacrifices out of 'love' for men. Does that not look like cruelty—or sadism? Or is it that he also is subject to a law of justice or to a destiny over and above himself? He requires our prayers but, except in a few very rare exceptions, he does not seem to care a straw or bother to reply. Is he powerless, then, to create a better world? If not, why has he willed or at least permitted it to be as it is, so unsatisfactory and with so little arrangement to promote the well-being or joy of his children? If the essence of love and of personal relations is dialogue why is this dialogue not *possible* with him in a genuinely interpersonal sense? This really was the complaint of Job—and not simply in a 'dialogic' monologue of blind faith.

Certainly, all sorts of theologies have tried to solve these and similar problems by refining both the answers and the very concept of God. Our question here, however, is whether an exclusively personal conception of the godhead does justice to it.

Finally, this God hides himself so well that one may, if one likes, deny his existence or act as if he did not exist without any unpleasant consequences. A single wrong note in chinese sacred music risked destroying the harmony of the universe, and the threat of death hung over anyone who dared to disturb 'canonical' harmony, similarly the man who in the christian Middle Ages spoiled or destroyed a sacred object, even a picture, was subject to severe penalties. Even a tiny disequilibrium in the intra-atomic world, imperceptible though it be to the senses, may run the risk of producing chaos in a vast portion of the universe. It is only God who can be manipulated without impunity? One can well understand that to 'save' God, Buddha elected to remain silent—by doing which, i.e. precisely by remaining silent, he discovered the *other* face of the Divinity, his apophatic, self-emptying, dimension : The 'no face'.

The question, then, is : Is there such a thing as an experience of God that does not lead to interpersonal dialogue? Can one conceive an authentic spirituality in which God is not a 'thou' for man nor his commandment the 'ultimate' of all perfection? In short, is the mystery of God exhausted in his unveiling as *Person*?

It is here that Hinduism, among other religions, has something to say. The Upaniṣads indeed point to a religious attitude that is not founded upon faith in a God-Thou, or a God-will-sovereignty, but in the supra-rational experience of a 'Reality' which in some way 'inhales' us into himself. The God of the Upaniṣads does not speak; he is not Word. He 'inspires'; he is *Spirit*.

In the personalist schema God is not simply the First Principle of things, the Cause of Being; he is Someone, he is a Person who calls to himself another person, is met, so to speak, face to face and is capable of either responding by love to another's love or refusing to do so.

In the schema of the Upaniṣads the main place is not given to call/response nor to acceptance/refusal. The basic categories here are knowledge and ignorance. The Absolute is discovered in its own realisation, i.e. in the experience in which it is attained. This meeting is not situated in the level of dialogue. Dialogue is itself transcended. Even the idea of meeting no longer enters the picture, for we are transferred to the sphere of union.

In its study of the diverse conceptions of the Divinity held by man the science of religions distinguishes between the concepts of God-immanent and God-transcendent which are at first sight opposed to one other. When we speak of God-transcendent we think immediately of a God who, *from on high*, summons, commands and directs. We then set such a God over against God-immanent who is *within us* and transforms us by incorporating us into himself.

In practice the modern West most often interprets the idea of transcendence in terms of pure exteriority—God the Other, God on high—and the idea of immanence in terms of pure interiority —a sort of divine presence within the soul, an 'inner' presence which leads in the final analysis to another exteriority, only in the opposite sense. In this conception, in fact, 'God within' transends the human subject no less certainly than does 'God without', the only difference being that, instead of situating *the Other* above, one now conceives him in another 'outside' that one calls 'inside'— which is the inexorable consequence of applying any form of spatial imagery to the mystery of God. We, in this system, become somehow *at the centre* : above, Transcendence, below, Immanence.

This conception of transcendence and immanence that makes God-transcendent 'exterior' and God-immanent 'interior', i.e. the soul's tenant, is however extremely narrow and limited. It is without doubt incapable of accounting for what the mystics of all times and of all culturo-religious contexts have experienced of the true transcendence and immanence of God.

Divine immanence, truly speaking, does not refer to a God who is, as it were, enclosed in our inner being, while at the same time irrevocably separated from us just like God in his transcendent or exterior aspect. Nor can true divine transcendence be reduced to the aspect of exteriority or even the 'otherness' of God. The authentic notion of transcendence surmounts all human barriers and situates God in the light inaccessible of which St Paul speaks, in the deep shadows of the Dionysian mystery-cult, on the other shore of the river, to use a phrase of the Upaniṣads or from the Buddha—in a word, beyond any 'real relationship'. Transcendence implies heterogeneity between God and man, and rejects any relatedness which is at the root of all religious anthropomorphism whether iconolatrous or personalist. True divine transcendence does not stem from the so-called natural and rational order; wherefore, if one is not willing to go beyond that order, one is unable, speaking absolutely, either to say or think anything about the Absolute.

Atheism, which denies all that human reason attempts to say about God beginning with his existence, is an eloquent spokesman for this divine transcendence. We must add at once that the atheist's critique, however purificatory it may be of man-made ideas of God, is for ever powerless to obliterate the pure diamond of absolute transcendence which is by very definition beyond all negation as well as beyond all affirmation.

Man's 'transit' to divine transcendence and even his discovery of it is only possible if the initiative comes from God's transcendence and is 'earthed' in his immanence. These two are like twin arches inseparable one from the other. One of them cannot hold without the other. Divine immanence is founded upon divine transcendence and *vice versa*. We might better still say that the bridge is less between man and God than between divine immanence and divine transcendence. Man is situated at the very heart of their complementarity or, better, reciprocal, intimacy— or rather he reaches both God and his own personal being in allowing himself to be penetrated by this divine dynamism.

If transcendence is truly transcendence, immanence is not a negative transcendence but a true and irreducible immanence. An immanent God cannot be a God-Person, 'someone' with whom I could have 'personal' relationship, a God-Other. I cannot *speak* to an immanent God. If I attempt to do so I cause this immanence to vanish because I am rendering it *other* and *exterior*. I cannot *think* of God-immanent for, if I try, I make him the *object* of my thought and project him before and outside me. God immanent cannot be someone existing or living in me, as if he were hidden or enclosed within me. Obviously, neither transcendence nor immanence is special, nor do they belong to any ontological category. To say with St Augustine that God is *intimior intimo meo* (more interior than my inmost being) is still insufficient to express true immanence, for God-immanent cannot be any *where*, beyond or behind, without his immanence vanishing. He is not *intimior*; the most one could say is that he is *intimissimum*. The immanence of God is something quite other than any notion of his 'dwelling' in us. God-immanent has no need of hiring a place in my soul or waiting patiently till I allow him a little spot 'within' where he may come and dwell. The idea of indwelling is merely a very pale and distant reflection of true immanence. Man is not the host of an immanent God. The traditional concept of 'God' is itself so linked by usage to the common notion of transcendence outlined above that it is only improperly speaking that the immanent aspect of the Absolute can receive the name of 'God'. For example, the name Creator attributed to God (to the transcendent God) cannot be predicated of the immanent Divinity, for how could it possibly create itself?

The Absolute is not only God in the sense of Other, Transcendent, Someone, a Person who is beyond and so Master, Lord, Creator, Father—terms, these, which correspond to the ideas of disciple, servant, creature, son—but, according to the terminology of the Upaniṣads it is also and quite as much *ātman*, the Self, *aham*, I, *brahman*, the ultimate Ground of everything. In a word, *God* and *brahman* are the same Reality seen as it were from two opposed perspectives, *God* being the summit and *brahman* the base of the triangle representing the Divinity.

We are thus confronted with the option of either reserving the name God to designate the dimension of transcendence, supremacy, otherness of the Absolute while finding another name such as *brahman, ātman*, Ground, Foundation to signify the dimension of immanence, or of enlarging the meaning of the word *God* to include also this second dimension. The first solution would undoubtedly simplify certain difficulties. It would clarify, for a start, the dialogue between so-called monotheistic religions which lean heavily upon the notion of transcendence and those others which stress more strongly the dimension of immanence. However, such a simplification even within the 'monotheistic' religions would not account for all the richness of their own traditions. One cannot ignore the sufism of islam and still less can one put to one side the mystical experiences of judaism and christianity.

If tradition were not already too burdened and the words Absolute and Divinity too abstract I should opt for reserving the word *Absolute* to designate the Supreme Reality as such and the words *God* and *Divinity* to signify respectively the transcendent and immanent aspects of that Reality. Let me, for the present anyway, use these terms in this way until such time as we come to consider the trinitarian mystery.

*   *   *   *

Is it possible to conceive a religion based exclusively on our 'relation' with the Divinity (immanent)? I do not think so, for the simple reason that no relationship is even conceivable with the Absolute as immanent, as has been explained above. Must we then exclude from religion the dimension of immanence? No, not that either. Is not this dimension of immanence like the horizon from which the God of the 'religions', the living and true God himself, emerges? And this is precisely the safeguard against his appearing merely as an idol and melting away in anthropomorphism. Is not this dimension of immanence like the hidden and always submerged bed of a river, like the stable floor over which the moving stream of existence flows, like the invisible air which sustains life, like the empty space which is a necessity for all communication, like the cosmic matrix without which the fecundation of nothingness could come to pass?

The unique relation that one can form with *brahman* consists in the rupture and negation of every alleged relation. Deep prayer is that of the creature who neither knows who does it nor that it is done. True confidence is that which is no longer conscious of depending on itself or on another or on nothing at all, for such an attitude would automatically engender dualism and thus a cleavage, as it were, through which doubt or mistrust could well infiltrate. In short, only the direct attitude, *ek-static*, that which in no way reflects upon itself, even to become conscious of itself, permits entrance into 'communication', or one might better say 'communion', with this ultimate ground of all things. This is basically what the *Māṇḍūkya Upaniṣad* calls the fourth state of consciousness, *turīya:*

'That which is neither internal consciousness
nor external consciousness,
nor both together;
which does not consist solely in compact consciousness,
which is neither conscious nor unconscious;
which is invisible, unapproachable, impalpable,
indefinable, unthinkable, unnameable,
whose very essence consists of the experience of its own self;
which absorbs all diversity,
is tranquil and benign,
without a second,
which is what they call the fourth state
—that is the *ātman*.'

(MandU 7)

One can prove, that is to say, demonstrate, the existence of God starting from certain premises : one cannot, however, prove the existence of *brahman*. *Brahman* is fact does not *ek-sist*. It is not the Creator, the origin of the *ek-sistential* tension between God and creature; *Brahman* has no *ek-sistence* because it possesses no *consistence*. If (to suppose the impossible) one succeeded in proving the existence of *brahman*, the result of this demonstration would, by very definition, be neither *brahman* nor Divinity.

The sole way of discovering *brahman* is by revelation in the sense of an unveiling of all the veils of *existence*, including that of the *ego*, i.e. of the one who undertakes the ascent, or rather the descent, in search of *brahman*. Thrusting towards the discovery of the ultimate foundation the *ego* cannot pursue the trail to the very end. If it tries, it inevitably disappears; it remains and survives only if it stops *en route*. 'He who returns only returns if he went half-way . . . (al-Misrī, referring to the ascension of Mahommed). Only the *aham*, the I, remains absolute, the one without a second, the *ātman*.

It is precisely this unveiling of the Divinity, the ultimate and immanent Ground of beings, to which the Upaniṣads make their essential witness. The rôle in the historical development of human consciousness seems to be to bring to human experience this extraordinary enrichment that contact with the immanent dimension of the Absolute imparts.

We have no right, naturally, to fail to recognise the other dimension, and the Upaniṣads certainly guard against this. There is no lack of theistic texts, especially in some of the Upaniṣads. We should also not forget that in the development of the religious consciousness of India they follow and complement the iconolatrous and personalist phase represented by the Vedas. A purely immanent spirituality would be still more false than one that is founded solely on 'transcendence' and regards the Absolute only as God, the Other, the Different, etc. Dualism and monism are equally false.

What we must stress most emphatically, in view of so many inadequate interpretations that are put forward both in the West and in the East, is that the central message of the Upaniṣads interpreted in their fullness (*seusus plenior*) is neither monism, nor dualism, nor the theism that is evidenced in some of them, but *advaita*, i.e. the non-dual character of the Real, the impossibility of adding God to the world or *vice versa*, the impossibility of putting in *dvanva*, in a pair, God and the world. For the Upaniṣads therefore, the Absolute is not only transcendent but both transcendent and immanent all in one.

The dimension of transcendence precludes a monistic identification, while that of immanence precludes dualistic differentiation. God *and* the world are neither one nor two. The fact that they are not two is as evident as the fact that they are not one. If they were one, one could not even speak of God, for only the world would then exist. Monism is atheism. If they were two, God would not be the Absolute, for the common 'element', the predicate of both, which includes both God and the world, would be superior to and more comprehensive than either—which is contrary to the definition of God as Absolute. It is readily understandable that more than one religion settles for speaking only of God—or of gods—but not of the Absolute.

Taken in isolation, these two propositions, *viz.* that God and the world are not two and are not one, do not pose a problem for thought. But it is quite otherwise when one envisages and seeks to understand them *together*. Left to itself human reason is inexorably checked when it attempts to resolve this problem. *A priori*, furthermore, we may make this affirmation. If reason were in fact capable by itself of unravelling the ultimate enigma of Reality it would be, by the very act, unequivocally divine—which would be tantamount to reducing reality to nationality. Reason cannot pass beyond the law of contradiction, and in order to arrive at the heart of this problem it is necessary to do so. We must here take careful note that this is not to say that the principle of contradiction is invalid nor that *advaita* is its contradiction or denial. It would be denied or 'contradicted' only if one were to say that God and the world are one *and* two (= not-one) at one and the same time. What *advaita* maintains is that God and the world *are not* either one thing or two different things, in short, neither one nor two : *an-eka, a-dvaita*.

Is there then another 'faculty' in man by which he can succeed in grasping the truth simultaneously of these two propositions and their inter-connection which is neither complementary nor simply reciprocal but, dare we say it, the truth of each immanent in the other? *Advaita vedānta* (and practically every mystic would agree) says that there is and calls it *anubhava*, experience, intuition and, at times, grace, faith, gift, revelation. When one has seen, felt, experienced that God is in all, that all is in God, that nevertheless God is nothing of that which is . . . then one is close to realisation, to the authentic *advaita* experience which, like all true experience, cannot be communicated or expressed by words, concepts or thoughts. The *Gītā* for example, says in its own succinct style :

> In Me all beings subsist
> but I do not subsist in them;
> yet in Me beings do not reside.
> Behold my divine mystery (*yogam aiśvaram*)
> I support yet do not reside
> in beings; my Self it is
> that causes beings to be (IX. 4–5).

The whole *śruti*, the hindu revelation, leads to this point and to this alone: to bring about the realisation that *ātman* is *brahman* (*ayam ātmābrahma*, *Māṇḍ. Up.* 2), that only *I* is (*abam asmi*, *Bṛhad*, *Up*, I, 4,1.), that my *me* is only *thou*, as we shall explain shortly.

We may say then that whereas dialogue, the prayer of praise and petition, along with love and the fulfilment of the divine will, are the basic religious categories of personalism, the essential attitudes of *advaita* will consist rather in silence, abandonment, total conformity, absolute non-attachment. *Advaita* spirituality rejects all anthropomorphism. For example, it is incapable of regarding sin as an 'offence' against God and it remains insensible to pious considerations such as would arouse compunction or gratitude in the heart of man by stressing the love that God shows him and what he has done or suffered on his behalf. All this, in the eyes of the *advaitin*, is sheer anthropomorphism. To thank 'the good Lord' for having created *me*, for having redeemed *me*, and other formulations of this type, seem to him the height of egoism, for they imply a reversal of the centre of gravity which thus passes from the Uncreated to the created. Nothing of that sort is compatible with the experience of the Absolute—according to a certain *advaita* spirituality.

Even the values which are recognised by both personalistic and *advaita* spiritualities take on a very different meaning according to whether they are lived out in the climate of the one or the other. In a personalistic spirituality contemplation consists above all in a more or less direct and loving gaze at the beauty, perfection and truth of the Other, which leads to a sort of *ecstasy of love*. In *advaita*, on the other hand, contemplation is simply the vision of total Reality where the 'ego' as such has no longer any place; it is the experience of the Absolute in its simplicity and its complexity, perfect joy attained in the *in-stasy of union*.

It is impossible to describe suitably a spiritual attitude that is, properly speaking, ineffable. It has sometimes been called the mystery of being, for it is best expressed in terms of 'being', but even the notion of being cannot do justice to the *advaita* experience.

The theist, on the one hand, has an experience of God as Other precisely because he starts from the subject *I* as a subject for the experience. The *advaitin* reverses the order. The Divinity cannot be described as Another because there is no subject I—at that level—to have the experience. For *advaita* the divinity is not something in me or outside me; for the *advaitin* experience is not something that *I* have. It is, rather, like a light in which the Real is illuminated and discovered. What the *advaitin* recognises is not his nothingness that is revealed *to* him but *the* Fullness which is unveiled in *itself*. There is thus no place for an *ego* in the *advaitin's* experience. There is no *ego* who has. It *is*, and that is all. All reversion to an *ego* would cancel out the *advaita* experience. It is ineffable because there does not exist any *ego* to describe it or witness it.

Jñāna-mārga, the way of knowledge, of pure contemplation, of ontological *theoria*, is the way *par excellence* of *advaita*. For the *advaitin* it is not a matter of transforming the world or even himself, as it is with the *karma-yogin*. Not for him is it a matter of worshipping God by loving him to the utmost, after the manner of the *bhakta*. It is sheerly a matter of forgetting himself, of yielding totally to God, thus even of renouncing loving him— a renunciation of love which does not proceed from a lack of love but is, on the contrary, more profoundly the sign of a love that is purer and 'carried further', a love which, having disappeared into the Beloved, has no longer any memory of itself. 'Stir not, stir not my love' (*Cant*. II. 7). There is no question here, of course, of dualistic knowledge. The *advaita jñāna* has no object, there is no limitation of knowledge. In fact, one cannot know the knower as an object (without converting it into a known in the process) (*Bṛhad. Up.* IV, 5, 15 and III, 4, 2). If one knows it, it is only by knowing with it, by being this knower, in this very knowledge. If the object does not exist, the subject loses its reason for being. However, can the subject itself be known without, by this very fact, being converted into the object of its own knowledge? Only a trinitarian answer provides the way out of this impasse.

II. THE TRINITY

One day at Rome during the Vatican Council some African Bishops confided to me their embarrassment at not being able to find in their own languages suitable words to convey the meaning of *nature* and *person* : the very concepts were unknown to those tongues. In reply I could only express my admiration for such languages, my regret at not knowing them myself and my hope that one day they would contribute notably towards the rejuvenation of the central body of dogma of christianity. However great in point of fact the value of conciliar and dogmatic formulations may be, they make no claim at all to encompass the totality of the divine reality which overflows their limits on all sides to an infinite degree. Furthermore, we must not forget that neither the actual words nor the concepts of *nature* and *person* are ever used in the New Testament to express the mystery of the Trinity and also that the first generations of christians lived out their faith in the Trinity without ever knowing them.

However that may be, my intention here is not to expound the doctrine of the Trinity; my desire is simply to show how in the light of the Trinity the three forms of spirituality described above can be reconciled. It is in actual fact only a trinitarian concept of Reality which permits us at least to indicate the main lines of a synthesis between these three apparently irreducible concepts of the Absolute.

The very popular 'modern' tendency to regard all *mystery* as *mysterious* (in its secondary meaning of *obscure and unfathomable*) has played a part in the trinitarian mystery—pure *light*—being relegated more and more to the list of objects and concepts considered virtually useless for a practical christian life (what is the good, if it is quite incomprehensible?), while in reality the Trinity is not only the theoretical foundation-stone of christianity but also the practical, concrete and existential basis of the christian life. This is not to say that the classic interpretation of the Trinity is the only one possible, nor even that it is impossible to transcend in theory the trinitarian dogma, but in that case one would have to find some comprehensive formulation which would subsume that which the Trinity now signifies. Christ refers time and again to someone greater than he, to Someone Else still to come; or, to put it another way, Christ has no meaning without a point of reference superior and anterior to himself. Openness in both directions—that is the pure algebraic expression of Christ as revelation of the trinitarian mystery, embracing both the human (the 'created') and the divine. But without pursuing this line of thought further—my aim at present is simply so to enlarge and deepen the mystery of the Trinity that it may embrace this same mystery existent in other religious traditions but differently expressed.

The Trinity, then, may be considered as a junction where the authentic spiritual dimensions of all religions meet. The Trinity is God's self-revelation in the fullness of time, the consummation both of all that God has already 'said' of himself to man and of all that man has been able to attain and know of God in his thought and mystical experience. In the Trinity a true encounter of religions takes place, which results, not in a vague fusion or mutual dilution, but in an authentic enhancement of all the religious and even cultural elements that are contained in each.

It is in fact in the Trinity that a true place is found for whatever in religion is not simply the particular deposit of a given age or culture. Only by a deepening of trinitarian understanding will such an encounter in depth come to pass, the synthesis and mutual fecundation of the different spiritual attitudes which comprise religions, without forcing or doing violence to the fundamental intuitions of the different spiritual paths.

It may be objected: Why do I persist, then, in still speaking of the Trinity when, on the one hand, the idea that I give of it goes beyond the traditional idea given by christianity and, on the other, by linking it closely with one particular religion, I thereby limit its scope, for a religion fits with difficulty into a schema that is not its own.

To this I reply: In the first place, there is, despite the development or deepening that takes place, a very real continuity between the theory of the Trinity that I outline below and christian doctrine. In the second place, I am convinced that the meeting of religions cannot take place on neutral territory, in a 'no man's land'—which would be a reversion to unsatisfactory individualism and subjectivism. It can take place only at the very heart of the religious traditions, on the assumption, of course, that they are not immobilised in a complete sclerosis. Thirdly, I am aiming at opening up a possibility of dialogue and am ready to start anywhere, if someone should offer me some other adequate take-off. Fourthly, it is scarcely possible to speak of these subjects from outside one or another tradition, for it is these very traditions that have determined the terminology. So in selecting one of them, I shall incur no criticism in choosing christian terminology as my point of departure. As for the the results, both our lives and dialogue have an open future before them.

THE FATHER

The Absolute is One. There is only one God, one Divinity. Between the Absolute or the One, God or the Divinity, there is no difference or separation : the identity is complete.

The Absolute has no name. All religious traditions have recognised that it is in truth beyond every name, 'un-namable', *a-nama*, *an-onymos*. The terms which describe it are simply designations which come from man and are always relative to man. One can call this Absolute *brahman* or one can call it *tao*. But *tao*, once named, is no longer *tao* and *brahman*, if known, is no longer *brahman*. The God that is seen is no longer the *God* (*o theós*) for no one has ever seen God; 'no one can see him and live'. His transcendence is constitutive and he alone is authentically transcendent.

In the christian tradition this Absolute has a definite designation : 'The Father of our Lord Jesus Christ'. It is he indeed whom Jesus called his Father and God and also taught us to call our Father and God. Yet neither the name Father nor the name God is the proper name of the Absolute. They are simply the names by which we *designate* him. He is our Father and our God, i.e. for us he is *Father* and *God*. But independently of us, in himself and for himself, what is He? Ultimately such a question does not even make sense. To ask what the 'self' of God is, surely involves an attempt in some way to go beyond his 'I' : the 'divine self' which could utter 'I'. The phrase 'God in himself' already implies a 'reflection' which presupposes already this ineffable God (whose 'self' we are asking for) and derives from there the notion of a 'self' of God which already has an origin and is thus no longer original and originating. God's re-flection is no longer the Father.

The Father is the Absolute, the only God, *o theós*. The Trinity is not a tri-theism. It is very significant that the first trinitarian formulae do not speak of the Father, the Son and the Spirit, but of the God, the Christ and the Spirit. Neither the Son nor the Spirit is *God*, but, precisely, the Son of God and the Spirit of God, 'equal' to the One God (*o theós*) as God (*theós*). At this point the inadequacy of the dialetic is clearly shown : neither the plurality nor, consequently, the equality is real. In the Absolute there is no plurality, no multiplicity, nothing which, multiplied or added, could be three ('He who starts to number starts to err', St Augustine says). For the same reason there is nothing in the Absolute that could be called equal or unequal. Where, indeed, in the Absolute could a point of reference be found which would permit the denial or affirmation of equality? One cannot say of the Son that he is equal to the Father any more than one can say that he is different. Any norm of measurement comes from outside, and outside the Absolute there is nothing. The same can be said as regards the Spirit. The Nicene Creed, as also the greek Fathers and even Tertullian, affirms that the 'substratum' of the Divinity resides in the Father. It is only with Augustine that the Divinity as the substratum which imparts unity to the Trinity begins to be considered common to the three persons.

A certain popular theological language which speaks of equality among the 'three' persons can certainly be accepted provided we stop short of accepting an objectified divine nature, 'trinitarianly' disincarnated, as it were (the famous rejected *quaternitas*). But this stopping to draw logical consequences sounds almost artificial, to say the least. The 'three' persons are 'equal' because all of them are 'God'; but this 'God' (whom they are supposed to equal) does not exist and is nothing outside or separated from the divine persons.

We would like here to approach the trinitarian mystery in a more direct way following up the more dynamic thrust of the greek patristic tradition and the latin bonaventurian scholastic.

Everything that the Father *is* he transmits to the Son. Everything that the Son *receives* he *gives* to the Father in return. This gift (of the Father, in the final analysis) is the Spirit.

Perhaps the deep intuitions of hinduism and buddhism, which come from a different universe of discourse than the greek, may help us to penetrate further the trinitarian mystery. After all, is not theology precisely the endeavour of the man of faith to express his religious experience in the mental and cultural context in which he is situated?

If the Father begets the Son (and this is a total generation since the Father gives himself fully to the Son) that means that what the Son is, is the Father, i.e., the Son is the *is* of the Father. In the formula of identity 'A is B' or 'F is S', what F is, is S. F, *qua* F, separately, in itself, *is not*. S is what F is. To the question : what is F? We must reply : it is S. To know the Son *qua* Son is to realise the Father also; to know Being as such implies to have transcended it in a non-ontical way.

Using other terms, we may say : the Absolute, the Father, *is not*. He has no *ex-sistence*, not even that of Being. In the generation of the Son he has, so to speak, given everything. In the Father the apophatism (the *kenosis* or emptying) of Being is real and total. This is what elsewhere I have called 'the Cross in the Trinity' i.e. the integral immolation of God, of which the Cross of Christ and his immolation are only the images and revelations.

Nothing can be said if the Father 'in himself', of the 'self' of the Father. Certainly he is the Father of the Son and Jesus addresses him as Father, but even 'Father' is not his proper name, though he has no other. In begetting the Son he gives up everything, even, if we may dare to say so, the possibility of being expressed in a name that would speak of him and him alone, outside any reference to the generation of the Son. Is it not here, truly speaking, in this essential apophatism of the 'person' of the

Father, is this *kenosis* of Being at its very source, that the buddhist experience of *nirvāṇa* and *śūnyatā* (emptiness) should be situated? One is led onwards towards the 'absolute goal' and at the end one finds nothing, because there is nothing, not even Being. 'God created out of nothing' (*ex nihilo*), certainly, i.e. out of himself (*a Deo*)—a buddhist will say.

Brahman is not, at this point the Upaniṣads contribute, certainly self-consciousness (which is the *ātman* realised). What the Father knows is the Son, but the expression is ambiguous and, as commonly understood, false, since the Son is not the accusative, the object of the Father's knowledge. He could then not be a person. Instead of saying: 'What, whom (*quod, quem*, in the accusative) the Father knows is the Son' it would almost be better to say—despite the violence done to the grammar— 'Who (*quod, quis* is the nominative) the Father knows is the Son.' The Son is not an object, he is the knowledge of the Father, since he is the Being, the *asti*, the *esti* of the Father. The 'identity' is total and the 'alterity' is equally total, infinite and absolute: *alius non aliud*, as the scholastics used to say.

One goes to the Father only through the Son. To go *directly to* the Father does not even make sense. If one tried to do so one would find that this so-called way to the Father is non-way, non-thought, non-being. Even the Son only knows the Father in being known by him: 'You are my Son; today I have begotten you', *'Aham asmī', 'ego eimi o eimī'*, 'I am who I am.' Creation is the echo of that divine primordial cry.

Any attempt to *speak* about the Father involves almost a contradiction in terms, for every word about the Father can only refer to the one of whom the Father is Father, that is, to the Word, to the Son. It is necessary to be silent. The most diverse religious traditions teach us that God is Silence. This affirmation must be accepted in its unfathomable profundity. God is Silence total and absolute, the silence of Being—and not only the being of silence. His word who completely expresses and consumes him, is the Son. The *Father has* no being the Son is *his* being. The source of being is not being. If it were, how could it be its source? *'Fons et origo totius divinitatis,'*—source and origin of the whole divinity.

In just the same way the idea suggested above that the Father is the unique and absolute I is inadequate and relative. The self-affirmation 'I' can only be made with reference to a Thou—a Thou which in its turn can only arise because there is a he. The Father *quoad se* in himself, is not even an I : he affirms himself only through the Son in the Spirit. He does not affirm himself, he affirms. Properly speaking no statement about the Trinity is true if taken in isolation from the other equally constitutive relations.

*   *   *   *

However, there exists in us a dimension—the deepest of all—that corresponds to this total apophatism. Not only does everything go to him but everything also comes from him, the Father of Lights. Undoubtedly one cannot reach him any more than a meteor can reach the sun without being volatilised and thus disappearing before getting there; but it is equally impossible to avoid being carried along in the current which draws everything towards him, the Father. One can be united *with* the Son or one may be *in* the Spirit but one can never *be* the Father, because the Father *is not*. One can never reach him because there is no 'end' to attain. And yet all things tend to him as their ultimate goal. The impossibility of reaching the Father is thus not an outhical, but a metaoutical impossibility.

Devotion to the Father meets an apophatism of Being; it is a movement towards . . . no place, a prayer which is always open towards . . . the infinite horizon which, like a mirage, always appears in the distance because it is no-where. The image, the icon, exists : the Logos. Being is only an image, a revelation of that which, if it were completely unveiled, would not even be, for being is its manifestation, its epiphany, its symbol. 'The Son is his name' says the gnostic *Evangelium veritatis* written out of a judaeo-christian milieu. 'The Son is the visibility of the invisible', St Irenaeus repeats.

'No one can come to me, if the Father who sent me does not draw him.' If we consider this statement in the light of what has just been said, it appears so evident that we could even take it for a tautology. How, indeed, could one reach the Son without participating in his sonship? But that sonship is real only because the Father causes it to emerge as such. It is, so to say, the reverse of paternity. If I go to the Son it is because I already participate in his sonship; in other words, because the Father has already included me in the sonship of his Son.

'He who has seen me has seen the Father' is another *mahāvākya* (great utterance) of the theology of the Father. Whoever sees Christ sees the Father because the Son is the Father made visible, because there is nothing else to see of the Father except the result of his paternity, namely, the Son. But to see the Son is to see him as Son of the Father and thus to see the Father in or rather through the Son (and not in himself since he is nothing). There are not two visions or seeings, one for the Son and another for the Father : whoever sees *me* in the see-ing of this *me* sees the *ego* which engenders it and gives it being. Strictly speaking one does not see *the* Son outside the Father nor the Father outside the Son. There are not two visions but one : *duo audivi, unum locutus sum* 'one thing God has spoken, two things have I heard' (*Ps.* 61 (62) 11).

'He who has seen me . . .'; only the Spirit can have such a 'vision' and with him those who live in the Spirit participate in this vision of the Father-Son. No-one goes to the Father except

C

through the Son and neither can anyone recognise the Son except in the Spirit. (*John* 14:17, 26; 15:26; 16:14.)

Properly speaking the spirituality of the Father is not even a spirituality. It is like the invisible bedrock, the gentle inspirer, the unnoticed force which sustains, draws and pushes us. God is truly transcendent, infinite. The moment that one stops, takes a stand, objectivises and 'manipulates' religion, faith and God, one destroys, so to speak, this ultimate ground of all things, which in itself is quite 'ungraspable' : one can recognise it as one's support. If hatred (lack of love) is the sin against the Son and blindness (denial of faith) the sin against the Spirit, despair (refusal to hope, being stubbornly shut up in the finite and limited) is the sin against the Father. The first can be pardoned. The second . . . well, it cannot be pardoned because one cannot ask forgiveness for it (as long as the sin remains). But the third is non-pardon itself, the sin against pardon (since all forgiveness is bound-less), the very contradiction of pardon. It is the sin of not wanting, not even being able to be pardoned. Bound fast by one's own limitations, one cannot tolerate the Father's causing his sun to shine both on the just and on the unjust and his rain to fall on good and bad alike. One attempts to imprison the liberty of God and of man, to limit the infinite, to shrink it and reduce it to the size of a creature who has continually denied his creaturely dignity, that is, of being an act *of* the Source. In other words, the sin against the Father is the break with the infinite, the denial of our divinisation, self-damnation in the finite, the closed and the limited : hell. Despair is the refusal of the infinite and suffocation in the finite . . . But man as far as he lives in time and space is not capable of absolute despair.

THE SON

It is the Son who is, and so *is* God. He is certainly *God-from* God and *Light-from* Light, but unless we proceed *ad infinitum* (and thus *ad absurdum* making God emerge from another Super-god and so on) we will have to say that the Father from which the *God-from* comes is properly speaking the Source of-God. This *of-God* is precisely the Son. It is the Son who acts, who creates. Through him everything was made. In him everything exists. He is the beginning and the end, the alpha and omega. It is the Son, properly speaking—and the Son was manifested in Christ—who is the Divine Person, the Lord. According to the most traditional theology the term Person cannot be used in the Trinity as a real analogy. 'Pluraliter praedicatur de tribus' says St Thomas referring to the divine persons (*S. Th*. I, q.39, a.3 ad 4). Analogy exists between the Creator and his creatures (*cf. vgr. S. Th*. I, q.13, a.5; q.29, a.4 ad 4), but not within the Trinity itself. 'Person' is not a 'universal' (*cf. S. Th*. I, q.30, a.4 for the *communitas negationis, intentionis rationis* and *rei*). Or in the intriguing words of Duns Scotus : *ad personalitatem requiritur ultima solitudo* (*Ordinatio* III, 1, 1, n.17). That which makes man a person is radical solitariness. An analogy always presupposes some foundation of the analogy (a *secundum quid unum*) entity or idea as the first point of reference, which in this case cannot exist outside the divine persons, for this would imply either a fourth ultimate principle or mere modalism if the difference between the persons were only in our mind; nor can it exist inside the divine persons, for this would imply real diversity and difference among them—always, of course, under the traditional assumption of considering persons as separate individuals. Thus, strictly speaking, it is not true that God is *three* Persons. 'Person' here is an equivocal term which has a different meaning in each case. Once the revelation of the living Trinity of Father, Son and Holy Spirit is received, it is already an abstraction to speak of 'God'. Divine 'nature', *God*, as a monolithic entity does not exist. There is no God except the Father who *is* his Son through his Spirit—but without three 'who's or 'what's of any sort. The word 'God' used of the Father, Son and Holy Spirit at once, is a *generic* name and therefore without concrete univocal content. There is not a *quaternitas*, a God-divine nature, outside, inside, above or beside the Father, the Son and the Holy Spirit. Only the Son is Person, if we use the word in its eminent sense and analogically to human persons : neither the Father nor the Spirit is a Person. There is no real analogous factor (*quid analogatum*) common to the Father, the Son and the Holy Spirit. For want of a better term one could certainly call them 'persons' in so far as they are real relative oppositions at the heart of the divine mystery, but one must beware of 'substantialising' them or considering them 'in themselves'. A person is never in himself, but by the very fact that he is a person is always a constitutive relation—a *pros ti*.

Correctly speaking, then, it is only with the Son that man can have a personal relationship. The God of theism, thus, is the Son ; the God with whom one can speak, establish a dialogue, enter into communication, is the divine Person who is in-relation-with, or rather, is the relationship with man and one of the poles of total existence. 'The name of God and Father, which is essentially subsistent, is his Logos'—says Maximus the Confessor (*Expo. orat. domin.* (PG 90, 871)). Or as the greek tradition liked to repeat with Dyonisius the Areopagite : God is 'neither triad nor monad'.

Now this God, the Son, is in trinitarian terminology the Mystery hidden since the world began, the Mystery of which the Scriptures speak, and which, according to christians, was manifested in Christ.

Here we must make a preliminary observation. Christ is an ambiguous term. It can be the greek translation of the hebrew Messiah, or it may be the name given to Jesus of Nazareth. One may identify it with the Logos and thus with the Son or equate it with Jesus. The nomenclature that I personally would like to suggest in this connection is as follows : I would propose using the word Lord for that Principle, Being, Logos or Christ that other religious traditions call by a variety of names and to which they attach a wide range of ideas. I am not making any claim here to solve the problem, and shall thus continue to use the name of Christ, for I believe it is important that the figure of Christ should regain its complete fullness of meaning, but I shall do so in a way that is devoid either of polemic or apologetic. Each time that I speak of Christ I am referring (unless it is explicitly stated otherwise) to the Lord of whom christians can lay claim to no monopoly. It is Christ, then, known or unknown—who makes religion possible. Only in the Lord is there 'religatio'. Christ, manifest or hidden, is the only way to God. Even by definition the unique link between the created and the uncreated, the relative and the absolute, the temporal and the eternal, earth and heaven, is Christ, the only mediator. Between these two poles everything that functions as mediator, link, 'conveyor', is Christ, the sole priest of the cosmic priesthood, the Lord *par excellence*.

When I call this link between the finite and the infinite by the name Christ I am not presupposing its identification with Jesus of Nazareth. Even from right within christian faith such an unqualified identification has never been asserted. What the christian faith does affirm is that Jesus of Nazareth is the Christ, viz., that he has a special and unique relationship with what Paul, following Old Testament usage, calls the Uncreated Wisdom, what John following Philo calls the Logos, what Matthew and

D

Luke following judaism consider in intimate relation with the Holy Spirit and what later tradition has agreed in calling the Son.

It is not my task here to discuss the other names and titles that have been accorded to this manifestation of the Mystery in other religious traditions. The reason I persist in calling it Christ is that it seems to me that phenomenologically Christ presents the fundamental characteristics of the mediator between divine and cosmic, eternal and temporal, etc., which other religions call *Iśvara, Tathāgata* or even Jahweh, Allah and so on—at least when they are not seeking to distinguish between a *saguṇa* and *nirguṇa* brahman. It is not without a deep and prophetic intuition that much of neo-hindu spirituality speaks in this way of 'christic awareness'.

Personalism is not wrong in asserting that personal relationship is essential to every evolved religious attitude and that the discovery or re-velation of the God-person is a decisive contribution of christianity. However, this affirmation needs to be completed by a recollection of the fact that the Father is 'greater' than the Son and that only in the Spirit is this interpersonal communion realised—and in a dialogue on an equal footing between *me*, man and *him*, God.

The Son is the mediator, the *summus pontifex* (High Priest) of creation and also of the redemption and glorification, or transformation, of the world. Beings *are* in so far as they participate in the Son, are *from, with* and *through* him. Every being is a *christophany* a showing forth of Christ.

If anthropomorphism is false, it is not at all because it assumes the human, but because it neglects the divine. That is to say, it is false in so far as it remains on this side of an authentic *theandrism*, completely divine and completely human at the same time, the end and fullness of all religion.

The Church is centred upon the authentic and living person of

Jesus Christ. Many view this as a limitation and conclude from this her inability to be in practice *a*, let alone *the*, universal religion. In actual fact the claim of the Church is not that she is *the* religion for the whole of mankind but that she is the place where Christ is fully revealed, the end and plenitude of every religion. Besides, it is not here that the limitation of the Church in fact consists. The real insufficiency of catholicity in its present-day historico-cultural situation derives far more from the fact that it has allowed these essential and authentically evangelical truths—that Christ *is* the Son, the Icon, the Image, the Word, the Glory, the very Being *of* the Father and that his Spirit is none other than the Holy Spirit—to be more or less eclipsed.

World religions, for their part, have not always paid enough attention to this dazzling, almost blinding revelation of the fullness of the divine mystery. They have thus preserved in their experience of the Absolute a sort of trinitarian indiscrimination. But is it not precisely this that has allowed them to maintain sometimes a perhaps more satisfactory equilibrium between these three essential dimensions of every spirituality that we have described above and that we may sum us as apophatism, personalism and divine immanence? Be that as it may, it is in the trinitarian possibilities of the world religions, in the striving of each in its own fashion towards the synthesis of these spiritual attitudes, that the meeting of religions—the *kairos* of our time—finds its deepest inspiration and most certain hope. The spiritual evolution of humanity is today passing through a particularly important stage and we have every reason to expect from it, as a result of the mutual fecundation of religions and of the experiences which undergird them, a fuller integration into human religious consciousness of the experience of the mystery and the life of the Trinity.

An analogy taken from the inner development of christian

spirituality will perhaps help us to grasp more fully the import of this *kairos*. At the very centre of christianity we discover an evolutionary process that could be described as the change-over from a *monodimensional supranaturalism* to a *supernatural naturalism*.

The impact on men of the message of the Gospel was such that in the early days of the Church he alone was considered a 'perfect christian who had already reached the *eschaton* (the end), that is to say, the martyr; or, in default of him, his substitute in the temporal sphere, the monk, the man who had passed beyond time, and who had renounced totally the world and all its works. It is very interesting here to observe that monastic acosmism, which in India gushed forth like an irresistible torrent as a result of the inner experience of the mystery of being, came into existence equally spontaneously in the West as a result of the eschatological experience in christian faith. Little by little, however, due not to the relaxation of the christian ideal, as some 'a-cosmics' will claim, but far more to a progressively growing awareness of and openness to the community of mankind, the world, nature and history, the christian, under the impulse of the Spirit guiding within, became more and more conscious of the necessity of penetrating to the very depth of both cosmic and human structures. He realised that it was his task to provide the leaven of which the Gospel speaks, to modify and transform them and thus to bring them at last to their perfect fulfilment in Christ—at the risk, certainly (not always overcome) of allowing himself to be swept away by the passing 'world'. Despite the great dangers and the number of those who succumb, the responsible christian who is sensitive to the movement of the 'wind' blowing from on high turns himself more and more in our day towards the world, towards an expansion of his life in the direction of others and the universe at large.

It would appear that there is nowadays a progressive abandonment not only of the life of the hermit or 'desert' but, equally, of the conventual life and the cloister, even of those more recent and more open forms of the classic religious life which developed during the last century. More than this, we can detect a thrust, as it were, of the Spirit pushing the christian forward beyond what we call 'christianity', beyond, I am tempted to add, even the institutional and visible Church. His ever more vivid awareness of the irresistible movement of all things towards the *apokatastasis*, the restoration, of all in Christ no longer permits him to confine himself by any barrier whatever at any level of thought or society or institutional life, but rather impels him in the Spirit to immerse himself at the deepest level in all endeavours related to man and this universe, just like the yeast which leavens the lump, the light which drives away shadows and the victim whose immolation saves and purifies all things.

Personal and special vocations will surely continue and nothing must be lost of all that the Church has garnered in the course of the centuries. Yet every vocation is of necessity a limited one and in a truly christian spirituality there is room for the most diverse vocations; but a-cosmism itself must become catholic and it is of vital importance that false a-cosmism should disappear, the acosmism which consists in shutting oneself up in a mental or institutional structure which, being the product of history, is destined by this very fact to be superseded in its turn by history. The signs of the times—and through them, the Spirit who reveals himself in them—invite us to open wide the doors of *oikoumene*, to break down the walls (of protection once upon a time, but nowadays of separation) of the so-called christian 'city' and to advance to meet all men with outstretched arms. They no longer permit a man to remain at the particularistic and limited, perhaps even sectarian and exclusive, level of his own 'individual' experience of Christ, for the only true experience of Christ is in human and cosmic *koinonia*. Furthermore, the experience of Christ and the spirituality which springs from it must expand in faith right up to their full trinitarian dimensions; than this nothing could be more in accordance with the teaching and example of the One who came to the world solely to witness to the Father, to accomplish not his own will but that of his Father who sent him, of the One who at the moment of his death, explained to his disciples that it was well for them if he went away, because otherwise the Holy Spirit, the teacher of all truth, would not come. If we remain attached exclusively to the 'Saviour', to his humanity and his historicity, we block, in a manner of speaking, the coming of the Spirit and thus revert to a stage of exclusive iconolatry.

Besides, these signs of the times are not only to be observed in christianity. Throughout the world, in actual fact, we are witnessing, the same process at work. World religions are 'secularising', new religions or quasi-religions, which aspire to embrace both the sacred and the profane, are springing up on all sides, while movements that claim to be a-religious are themselves becoming more and more sacralised. And the Son, the Lord under whatever name, is the symbol for this process.

THE SPIRIT

The revelation of the Father is the revelation of God transcendent—of such a transcendence that, strictly speaking, even the name of God cannot be attributed to him. Thus, for us, pilgrims as we are in space and time, it is the Logos that is God. The revelation of the Spirit, on the other hand, is the revelation of God immanent. As was explained above, the divine immanence is not simply a negative transcendence; it is quite a different thing from the divine welling in the depths of the soul. Essentially it

signifies the ultimate inner-ness of every being, the final foundation, the *Ground* of Being as well as of beings.

Properly speaking, the concept of revelation can be applied
only to the Son. Transcendence as such cannot reveal itself—nor,
similarly, can it be incarnated, which amounts to the same thing—
since that which reveals itself is no longer transcendence but the
revelation *of it*, i.e. God, the Son, the Logos, the Icon.
Transcendence needs to reveal itself in order to manifest itself, to
make itself known, but for that precise reason when it manifests
itself it ceases to be transcendence and becomes revelation, the
manifestation of the transcendent. In a way that is analogous,
revelation of immanence has no meaning at all, strictly speaking,
for if immanence is to reveal itself, that implies that it is not immanent but underlying (since it had to be revealed). Transcendence ceases to be when it reveals itself : immanence is incapable
of revealing itself, for that would be a pure contradiction of
terms ; an immanence which needs to manifest itself, to reveal
itself, is no longer immanent. Hence the extreme difficulty of
using all these categories outside their own terms of reference.
Therefore I am choosing here the language appropriate to
meditation, such as springs from the intelligence by a contempla-
tive affinity.

Divine immanence is first of all a *divine* immanence : God is
immanent to himself, and it is only God who can be immanent to
himself. Divine immutability is something quite different from
static immobility. Doubtless God does not move as creatures do,
but he is not immobile as they are either. That is why in the
bottomless ocean of the Divinity there is a sort of constant deepening, of permanent 'interiorisation'. It is the experience of the
trinitarian mystery which shows us that in reality God is
immanent to himself, that there is in him a sort of bottomless
interiority, infinitely interior to itself

When one seeks to penetrate the innermost mystery of a being, piercing its surface and going always deeper, one passes one after another successive levels of the within-ness of this being to itself. Finally there comes a moment when it seems that one has passed and left behind the very specificity of this being, its 'self'. Then, (if it is permitted thus to symbolise this experience) one only meets—for there no longer exists anything else—on the one hand God and, on the other, *nothing*, nothingness. If now one uses the same metaphor when one seeks to plumb the final secret of God, one finds that at the deepest level of the Divinity what there is is the Spirit. To continue speaking in images—only dangerous when one stops with them—could one not say that in spite of every *effort* of the Father to 'empty himself' in the genera-tion of the Son, to pass entirely into his Son, to give him every-thing that he *has*, everything that he *is*, even then there remains in this first procession, like an irreducible factor, the Spirit, the non-exhaustion of the source in the generation of the Logos? For the Father the Spirit is as it were, the return to the source that he is himself. In other, equally inappropriate, words : the Father can 'go on' begetting the Son, because he 'receives back' the very Divinity which he has given up to the Son. It is the immolation or the mystery of the Cross in the Trinity. It is what christian theologians used to call the *perichoresis* or *circumincessio*, the dynamic inner circularity of the Trinity.

It must be said immediately, moreover, that this divine im-manence which is the Spirit is equally the divine immanence of the Son. The Spirit is the communion between the Father and the Son. The Spirit is immanent to Father and Son jointly. In some manner the Spirit 'passes' from Father to Son and from Son to Father in the same process. Just as the Father holds nothing back in his communication of himself to the Son, so the Son does not keep to himself anything that the Father has given him. There is nothing that he does not return to the Father. Thus the trinitarian cycle is completed and consummated, though in no way is it a 'closed cycle'. The Trinity is, indeed, the real mystery of Unity, for true unity is trinitarian. For that reason, properly speaking, there is no *Self* in the reflexive sense. The *Self* of the Father is the Son, his *in-himself* is the Spirit. But the Son has no *Self*; he is the Thou of the Father; his *Self* in relation to his Father is a Thou. Similarly with the Spirit; the Spirit 'in himself' is a contradiction. There is only the Spirit *of* God, of the Father and Son. He is the One sent. He is neither an I who speaks to another, nor a Thou to whom someone else speaks, but rather the *we* between the Father and the Son—that we which encompasses also the whole universe in a peculiar way. Strictly speaking one cannot even say that the Father is an I, if one takes it to be a sort of 'absolute subject'. The Son is assuredly the Thou of the Father. Furthermore, the Son is the Word. The speaker is known only in the Word. He is nothing outside this speaking which is his Son. This is why in relation to us the divine I appears only in the *thou* of the Logos through the *we* of the Spirit. There is no room for egoism in the Trinity. It has no *Ding an sich,* selfhood as such.

The themes upon which we are now touching are, without doubt, most delicate ones, which no one has the right to approach without reverent awe, deep humility and a sincere respect for tradition. Yet is it not precisely this respect for tradition, this awe and humility which oblige us to bring all our faith to bear upon an examination of them? If we take seriously the apophatism of the Father, we are able only to say that the Son is the Thou of the Father, without even being able to add that the Father is *an I*. He is an I who is totally out-spoken, that saying all that he is in his word, there is nothing left in him. This is why in relation to us it is the self-same Logos which appears to us as the divine I.

D*

The Trinity is neither modalistic nor tri-substantial (tri-theistic). We must always bear in mind that modalism is very difficult to avoid when, in an attempt to explain trinitarian mystery, one starts with the idea of being, thus identifying by a single equation Being and God. If in fact there is a single God, there can only be a single Being and since in that case the three Persons cannot be three beings, there is no alternative other than for them to be 'three' participants in Being, a Being that shares itself in *three* 'perspectives' internal to its very Being. But in this case either the 'perspectives' are real and thus each of them does nor comprise the whole of Being (which would deny the Divinity of each of the three Persons) or they are not real and then modalism again creeps in (for in that case the Persons are only different modes of Being itself).

The traditional answer to this problem is that the Persons are subsisting relations, which is the same as saying that Being is relation, both to the interior of itself and to what is exterior, with the result that beings are only relational games. Viewed from this angle what becomes of the notion of substance? Granted, in God there are not three substances but three persons. However, what is divine substance? Is there *one* divine substance? It could not in actual fact exist outside Persons. It cannot be considered as a thing, a common *sub-stance* in which the persons *participate*, since each person cannot form *part* only of whatever that would be, as personal divinity is complete.

The *advaita* which helps us express suitably the 'relation' God-World is again a precious aid in elucidating the intra-trinitarian problem. If the Father and the Son are not *two*, they are not one either : the Spirit both unites and distinguishes them. He is the bond of unity; the *we* in between, or rather within.

The Father has no name because he is beyond every name, even the name of Being. The Spirit has and can have no name either because he is a certain way on this side of every name, even that of Being. Being and beings—and hence all existence—belong to the kingdom and sphere of the Son. If, as the Council of Toledo says, the Father is *fons et origo totius divinitatis*, source and origin of the whole divinity, if the Son *is* God and, as the greek Fathers say, developing the image, the River who flows from the Source, then the Spirit is, as it were, the End, the limitless Ocean where the flux of divine life is completed, rests and is consummated (*plenitudo et pelagus totius divinitatis*). So long as the Spirit has not been received, it is impossible to understand the message brought by the Son and, equally, to reach *theosis*, the divinisation that the Spirit realises in man. There is no doubt that hindu thought is especially well prepared to contribute to the elaboration of a deeper theology of the Spirit. Indeed, is not one of its fundamental urges precisely this, to rise and strive towards the discovery and realisation of the Spirit—striving and thrusting in a way that is worthy of admiration and often inspired, though sometimes, also, tragic?

One cannot have 'Personal relations' with the Spirit. One cannot reach the Transcendent, the Other, when one is directed towards the Spirit. One cannot pray *to* the Spirit as an isolated term of our prayer. One can only have a non-relational union with him. One can only pray *in* the Spirit, by addressing the Father through the Son. It is rather the Spirit, who prays in us. When one embarks on the way of the Spirit, one can only reach the extraontic foundation of everything. But the foundation of Being is no longer Being.

It is to this Spirit that most of the upaniṣadic assertions about the Absolute point, when seen in their own deepest light. One could cite almost every page of the Upaniṣads for examples. Indeed what is the Spirit but the *ātman* of the Upaniṣads, which is said to be identical with *brahman*, although this identity can only be existentially recognised and affirmed once 'realisation' has been attained? 'In the beginning was the Logos' the *New* Testament affirms. 'At the end will be the *ātman*' adds the wisdom of this *cosmic* Testament to the canon that is not yet closed. The *end* of every individual is the recognition that this *ātman* is identical with *brahman*. Man finds himself, as it were, under the arc which stretches between the transcendent God and the immanent Divinity. The Mediator (unknow by his name) is the one who unites by the 'supreme bridge' (*pontifex maximus*) *ātman* and *brahman* : One could translate in this way a well-known Sanskrit verse : 'He who knows that *brahman* exists—his is an indirect knowledge; he who knows "I am *brahman*"—his is a direct knowledge'. 'I am *brahman*' is so far as it is not *brahman* who says so. The one who can speak thus does it only as the Spirit and the Word who is thus spoken is the Logos.

*　　　*　　　*　　　*

The spirituality of the Spirit is quite different from that of the Word. One attains the Spirit neither by word nor by action. Faith in the Spirit cannot be clothed in personalist structures. It does not consist in the discovery of Someone, and even less in dialogue with him. It consists rather in the 'consciousness' that one is not found outside reality, in the 'realisation' that one is, so to speak, included in it, that one is already *there*, that one is (if we prefer to put it this way) known to and loved by it—better still, that one is as though enveloped, submerged in knowledge and love, in the beauty that one has with joy penetrated. It is a kind of total passivity : there is no longer any *me* to save, for one has grasped that there is an I who calls one by a new and completely hidden name. The spirituality of the Spirit shows us in the mystery the horizon on which the I emerges—an I which is not at all the Spirit, but which is the Father through the Son. Only the spirituality of the Spirit makes this discovery possible and for this very reason the 'name' is always new and hidden. Its only way is the way of silence—the silence of words no doubt but also that of desires, that of action, the silence, finally, of being, of wishing to be, the total silence of the will to be—because it is neither through flesh nor blood nor the will of man that one becomes what one *is* (what one *will be*, for one who is situated on the temporal plane). Faith in the Spirit cannot be formulated; it too is silent.

Life according to the Spirit is authentic existence. This is why, until the end has *arrived*, it cannot be lived in a total way. It needs to be complemented by the other spiritualities, especially that of the Incarnation. This complementarity does not mean that the ways of the Word and of the Spirit are not complete in themselves but demonstrates the fact that temporal human existence is conditioned by the lack of unity between the way of the Word and that of the Spirit. The function of a perfectly balanced spirituality is precisely to integrate the one with the other. The way of the Spirit, indeed, without its trinitarian integration carries a certain risk of disincarnation. One does not, hoewever, have the right to treat the negative or apophatic way which is constitutive of the spirituality of the Spirit as disincarnation or 'spiritualism'. Since the Spirit is sanctifier and purifier the way of the Spirit can only be spoliation and negation of all that is not yet. It is necessary constantly to deny everything *creaturely* in order to accomplish the transformation. The upaniṣadic expression of this spirituality is *neti neti*. One must not be afraid of negation. Everything that *can* be negated is still, by that very fact, mere potentiality of being and consequently *is not*. Being, which really *is*, *cannot* be negated —any more than the principle of contradiction can be contradicted, without a prior supposition. It is possible to deny being but not to negate it, destroy it, injure it in any way. Suicide is only possible for the mortal, but being is immortality. The fear of total negation of self (as demanded by all true asceticism—which negation can only be realised in and through the Spirit) is clear proof that this *self* which is afraid is not the real and authentic *thou*. The only one who seeks to 'be a man' is one who is not, the adolescent, for example, or the vain. He who is really a man does not concern himself with *appearing* so. One may as well hasten to disencumber oneself of that which one is afraid to lose. This very fear is the sign of the non-value of what one is afraid to lose. 'Life' which can be lost is not Life. Nor is existence which *can* be lost real existence. To relinquish all his 'substance' for the sake of love (which is stronger than death) is a mere trifle for the one who truly loves. True asceticism begins by eliminating the fear of losing what can be lost. The ascetic is the one who has no fear.

It is the Spirit, which situates us in the only true perspective, altering all those perspectives from which, by reason of our creaturely and, moreover, fallen condition, we are accustomed to view things. Only in the Spirit is true *metanoia*, conversion, return, change of *noûs* (mind) and *gnosis* (knowledge). It is not only our moral 'values' that the Spirit alters, not only our natural vision of things that it transforms, but it also renews in us 'religion' and spirituality. The Spirit comes only after the Cross, after Death. It works in us the Resurrection and causes us to *pass* to the other shore.

The inversion that the Spirit brings about is total. The wisdom of this world becomes folly and the mystery of the Cross the true wisdom. The Spirit leads man to realise that he is not an I (*ego*) but a thou (*te*); that he is only in so far as the one I (*ego*, *aham*) says to him *thou* :

'I have called thee in justice' (Isaiah 42 : 6);

—never in the nominative, which is not even possible, but
—in the vocative, to give him *his* very being, which is being
called (to existence) :

'Thou art my Son; today I have begotten thee (Ps. 2 : 7);

—in the accusative, for he calls him to an intimate relationship :

'I have called thee' (Isaiah 42 : 6);

—in the dative, for he entrusts to him the task of gathering all
men into community :

'I have given to thee the peoples' (Ps. 2 : 8); and completes in
him the universe :

'I have purposed you for a light to the nations and a bond of
union to the peoples' (Isaiah 42 : 6 & 49 : 6);

and finally

—in the ablative, for he uses him as an instrument for the ser-
vice of the world and the completion of creation :

'to open the eyes of the blind' (Isaiah 42 : 7).

It is the Spirit who gives an understanding of the Scriptures.
The Spirit, for example, causes us to understand that, when it is
written for our dull ears and stony hearts that 'the Word was
made flesh', it is in reality the flesh which is made Word—for
the descent of God, as St Thomas would say, cannot be real,
whereas on the contrary our own ascent to divinity can be
absolutely real. This is true, moreover, not only for us but also
for the Word, about whom one cannot with any truth assert that
having passed in tranquillity and repose innumerable aeons of time
in his heaven he decided one fine day to 'descend' here below. The
real truth is that he—sole begotten of the Father—was *a 'prin-
cipio' aeternitatis*, the first born of Creation, the first Principle
of all things even before the foundation of the world, the Lamb
immolated since the origin of time. For what in very truth is

Creation if not an invitation to enter into the mystery of God through Christ in the Spirit?

In so far as man has not had the experience, in one way or another, of being a Thou spoken by God, in so far as he has not discovered with the wonder of a child (because it is full of mystery) that he *is* precisely because the I calls him (and calls him by his name, the name representing here his self-hood, his being) he has not yet reached the depth of life in the Spirit. The Spirit causes us to cry *Abba, Father,* because in the last analysis there is only a Thou of the Father, which is the Son. The Father calls us with the same 'calling' with which he calls his Son. In God there is no multiplicity. There cannot be two 'callings' nor two 'words' in God. We *are* only in so far as we *participate* in the Logos. Every being is, and is only, a *christophany.*

The Augustinian 'psychological' conception of the Trinity is well known : we *are,* we *know,* we *will* (or *love*) : I *am* knowing and loving, I *know* myself as being and loving, I *will* to be and to know (cf. *Conf.* XIII, 11—an inspired conception most certainly and one which enables us to approach the divine mystery by taking as our starting-point man, the image of the Trinity in the innermost and truest part of his being. Yet in spite of its validity its anthropocentricity is very obvious : the Father, Being; the Son, Intellect; the Spirit, Love, *mens, notitia amor* or also *memoire, intelligentia, voluntas*).

Now what we would venture to suggest—with the Gospel in hand and at heart—is the Father, Source, the Son, Being, the *Thou*; and the Spirit, Return to Being (or Ocean of Being), the *we.* Paul's trinitarian formulation of God '*above* all, *through* all and *in* all' (Eph. 4 :6) gives us the clue :

Epi pántōn—over all, *super omnes,* the Source of Being, which is not Being, since, if so, it would be Being and not its source : the ultimate *I.*

Dià pántōn—through all, *per omnia*, the Son, Being and the Christ, he through whom and for whom everything was made, beings being participants in Being: the *Thou*—still scattered in the many *thous* of the universe.

En pāsin—within all, *in omnibus*, the Spirit, divine immanence and, in the dynamism of pure act, the end (the return) of Being. For that reason Being—and beings—only exists in so far as it proceeds from its Source and continues to flow in the Spirit: the *we*, in as much as it gathers all of us, who were mostly 'he, they' into the 'integrated communion of that perfect reality.

III. THEANDRISM

Theandrism is the classical and traditional term for that intimate and complete unity which is realised paradigmatically in Christ between the divine and the human and which is the goal towards which everything here below tends—in Christ and the Spirit. For that reason the term seems to me particularly well suited to characterise the synthesis of the three spiritual attitudes described above and also the three spiritualities developing from them, called respectively the ways of the Father, the Son and the Spirit.

I prefer the term *theandric* to the term *trinitarian* to describe this synthesis and the whole catholic (*kath'holon*) spirituality in which it culminates. The first reason for this is that current theology has too often relegated the trinitarian mystery to the exclusive sphere of the Divinity, 'theology' in the greek use of the word, i.e. the study of God-in-himself totally or almost independent of the 'economy' or study of God in his 'temporal manifestation', i.e. creation and incarnation. A *trinitarian* spirituality in the strict sense of the word might run the risk of not conceding, or at least of not sufficiently manifesting, the necessity of the dimension of incarnation, of humanity, without which every synthesis remains inevitably impoverished. Another reason for avoiding this term is that, since the Trinity is the central dogma of christianity, it is in christian faith where this essential mystery of the divine life, even of the whole of reality is thematically

developed, whatever the 'adumbrations' of it that may be dis-
cerned elsewhere, while I would prefer a term without such direct
christian connotations.

The term theandrism indicates with sufficient clarity these two
elements of every spirituality : the human element which serves
as the point of departure and the transhuman factor which gives
it inner life and is its transcendent result. I do not deny that my
interpretation of theandrism is in fact both trinitarian and
christian, but what I wish to make very clear is that this
theandrism is not a concept inherent in and introduced by christian faith alone but that it is already present as the end towards
which the religious consciousness of humanity tends, and also as
the most adequate interpretation of mystical experience (which is
itself the culmination of all religious experience). Christ is at one
and the same time God and Man. Nestorianism, as also mono-
physism, mutilates him, 'drains' him—'lest the cross of Christ be
emptied (*kenōthē* 'evacuetur' 1. Cor. 1 :17) as St Paul says. Christ,
the Man, is Jesus and even, eschatologically speaking, all that
which is created. Christ is God, he is the Son of the Father and his
Spirit is the Holy Spirit. It would destroy the whole mystery to
envisage in separation from one another—even more so live—
the apophatism and transcendence of the mystery of the Father,
the immanence and fullness of the mystery of the Spirit and the
homogeneity to man of the personal mystery of Christ.

'Who aspires to play the angel plays the ass' Pascal used to say.
Could we not add to this aphorism, 'Who aspires to play the ass
can never succeed', for the divine light shines in us and on us, it
envelops us and transforms us from within ('the light of thy face
has marked us, O Lord'). Furthermore 'who aspires to play the
man' (and only man) inevitably plays the ass (in the Pascalian
sense of the words) because man is much more than a 'thinking
reed'. Man, indeed, infinitely surpasses mere 'man'. His being

cannot be reduced to a theoretical 'pure nature' which would have its own goal and would require a fresh intervention of God to raise it to a so-called supernatural state. The 'vocation' which summoned man into being destined him from the very beginning to be the Son of God, one with the only Son. To consider man simply as a 'reasonable animal' is tantamount to refusing him the right to his own true goal and depriving him utterly of the hope of ever attaining it. Or, we might say, it is to alienate him, to make him other than what he is by aspiration and divine calling, other (in a word) than *man*; it is to impose upon him a destiny and a calling that is not his. I find it impossible not to see in fact a sort of 'alienation' of man in this artificial conception of the supernatural mentioned above. It is no doubt a result of his greek heritage that western man is so chary when it comes to the question of recognising the divine in man. There is a fear, even an anguish of mind, lest man lose his individuality. Yet does not man mutilate himself still more dangerously by refusing to recognise within himself that innermost core which lies deeper than anything he can attain by his mere reason?

In the psychological and anthropological sphere the meaning of theandric spirituality is clear. It maintains a harmonious synthesis to the greatest (though not necessarily best) extent between the tensions and polarities of life : between body and soul, spirit and matter, masculine and feminine, action and contemplation, sacred and profane, vertical and horizontal—in a word, between what one may continue to call divine and what one has been accustomed to call human.

The difficulty arises, however, when one turns to the sphere of theology proper. Upon what image of man, on the one hand, and of God, on the other, are we to rely for inspiration in order to arrive at this synthesis?

Here we might say that the fundamental insight of theandrism

consists in the realisation that man possesses an infinite capacity
which links him up to the asymptotic limit called God; or, to put
it the other way round, that God is the end, the limit of man.
In other words, theandrism is in a paradoxical fashion (for one can
speak no other way) the infinitude of man, for he is tending
towards God, the infinite, and the finitude of God, for he is the
end (*finis*) of man.

A theandric spirituality succeeds in avoiding anthropomorphism on the one hand and 'theologism' on the other. It seeks to re-
establish a non-dualist vision of these two poles of reality which
become blurred and vanish when one considers them in isolation
the one from the other. A purely empirical down-to-earth
anthropology degrades man, while an exclusively 'revelational'
theology destroys God himself. Man and God are neither two nor
one. Theandrism is that intuition which the majority of thinkers
of all ages have grasped and set forth, though in doing so frequently they have stressed by way of reaction one of the poles
more than the other, or have used very diverse terminologies
which admittedly are incapable of supporting the tension between
these two poles of reality. The proper balance of the scales is
upset when one ceases to look at the centre; if one gazes at God
one is blinded, if one gazes at man one is deafened.

The negative aspect of a theandric spirituality is relatively easy
to describe. It is a matter of re-establishing equilibrum, or rather
unity, of 'distinguishing' in order to unite, of realising that a uni-
lateral and exclusive vision of the bi-polar nature of reality is always limited and thus insufficient. It is a matter of understanding
that an integral anthropology implies a humanist theology.

The positive working-out of a theandric vision of reality is a
task that our day needs to accomplish. It is not sufficient to
acknowledge an openness or undefined relation in some human
or cosmic reality; it is a question also of discovering the guide-

lines and vectors of the sum-total of the data, without aiming of
course at offering more than a paradigm. To say that empirical
man is 'contingent' or insufficient and to add the complementary
and unqualified assertion that God is 'necessary' and wholly
sufficient will not do. To do so would be both to misconstrue man
and postulate an artificial *deus ex machina*. It is not a question of
imperfect man on the one side and perfect God on the other, but
rather—existent at all times and in all situations—a theandric
reality. A 'purely transcendent' God is an abstraction of the same
sort as a 'purely independent' man. There are not two realities :
God *and* man (or the world); but neither is there one : God *or*
man (or the world), as outright atheists and outright theists are
dialectically driven to maintain. Reality itself is theandric ; it is
our own way of looking that causes reality to appear to us sometimes under one aspect and sometimes under another because our
own vision shares in both.

God and man are, so to speak, in close constitutive collaboration for the building-up of reality, the unfolding of history and
the continuation of creation. It is not a case of man toiling here
below and God surveying him from on high, with a view to giving reward or inflicting punishment. There is a movement, a
dynamism, a growth in what christians call the mystical Body of
Christ and buddhists call *dharmakāya*—to give just two examples.
God, man and the world are engaged in a unique adventure and
this engagement constitutes true reality.

I would make one final remark. Relativity is not the same as
relativism, we have been presupposing all the time. If I emphasise
the relativity of spiritualities and religions, as also of the basic
human attitudes that underlie them, it is out of no desire to level
out everything and reduce it to a sort of amorphous equalitarian-
ism. Nor do I pass judgement in any way at all.

The man who is satisfied and convinced in his own fundamental human way of life (religion, spirituality, etc.) must follow it without tormenting himself with useless scruples. It would be fatal for him if a false striving towards artificial perfection produced in his conscience inhibitions and repressions which are invariably pernicious. It is always far better to be a good atheist or a convinced buddhist than an indifferent or bad muslim or an insincere hindu. Furthermore, it would be absolutely mistaken to attack the buddhist, for example, and his beliefs as if they were adversaries in warfare. So long as the buddhist finds in his belief a satisfying answer to his fundamental problems, it would be immoral to cause him in the name of an alleged objectivity to have doubts, for man always reaches truth in a relative fashion. The synthesis that we look for and that permits each religion and each believer to come in theandric synthesis to the plenitude and perfection of faith and mystical experience is of a totally different kind. I am alluding here to nothing less than a new self-awareness, so to say, on the part of humanity, of which the beginnings and tentative outlines have been glimpsed for some time but which now is unveiled little by little before our astonished eyes. This it is, without a shadow of doubt, that constitutes the so urgent *kairos* of the moment of history that we are in the process of living.

I do not intend, however, in these last pages to embark on a study of this *theandric synthesis* of the different spiritualities or mystical ways that I have cursorily described. I prefer rather to give an idea and explanation of it by a reverse procedure, by pointing out the basic deviations that threaten each of these three ways if they are followed exclusively and without the necessary cross-references between one and the other. Every sort of particularism, in fact, which limits itself to one or another of these attitudes, neglecting the other two and defying their complementary and

essential interconnection, will lead inevitably to a rigid and uni-
lateral spirituality.

NIHILISM

There is no doubt that one of the most effective jolts that the
western world is experiencing nowadays comes from nihilism.
Without doubt our time revolts, often with violence, against the
existential idolatry that is to be found, so it would seem, in all
religions of every sort. Modern man cares very little in point of
fact whether the idol is the *true* God and the formulas dealing
with it *true* formulas (is there not more reality, and hence
divinity, in an idol of stone when sincerely adored, for example,
than in the mere concept of the Trinity, when not re-enacted by
a living faith?). Consequently, a growing number of men of un-
deniable intellectual and moral worth reject and deny the
traditional affirmations of the religions concerning the existence
and nature of God. In a word, the world is in process of discovering the positive value of atheism.

Basically it is a thirst for the Absolute in man that is at the
root of the nihilist climate of thought in our day. God cannot
be *exclusively* an idol, nor an alibi nor simply a person, nor the
Other *par excellence* nor even the Supreme. It is the very fact
that he takes with full seriousness his awareness of his fundamental truth that drives modern man to this impassioned search
beyond everything that has existence, causing him to reject all
that is only intermediary and to refuse inexorably all *vain* con-
solation, all *reward*, all recompense, all hope. Indeed all religious values, presented as they too often are without sufficient
reference to the totality of the mystery, appear to him just decep-
tive and inferior remedies merely useful for immature and under-
developed mentalities.

No indeed, they are not so far from the truth, these nihilists who claim that nothing-ness, a complete void, is the last word in the mystery! They are not outside the *oikoumene*, these atheists who reject the god-idol so often worshipped by the religions of the world. Rather are they the present-day witnesses to a spirituality which was directed to the Father but to a Father 'severed' from the living Trinity. They are bearing witness to the truth that no one can ever see the Father, because, in the final analysis, there is *nothing* to see.

It must be added that neither atheism as a doctrine nor nihilism as a 'spirituality' can be accepted as being that definitive religious attitude which mankind is now in process of gestating and for which it earnestly longs. They do, however, represent a dimension which must be integrated into that total synthesis which we have called theandrism. After all, was there not a time when it was the christians who were called atheists precisely because they rejected the gods?

Another example of this spiritual dimension can be found in buddhism, at least in the buddhism of one particular sort. It would appear that it is in the spirituality of the Father that such a buddhism is invited to find its integration. In a theandric spirituality buddhism finds its true place, but it stresses power-fully that to speak of the ultimate mystery makes *non-sense*, that to manipulate the Supreme, even with our intelligence, is a blasphemy and that silence is the base and source of all speech, all thought and all being.

HUMANISM

It is not by chance that the most characteristic crypto-heresy of the west since the Middle Ages has been and still is humanism. Of this the explanation is simple. On one side humanism is a healthy reaction against an excessive emphasis on eschatology and a certain anti-natural supernaturalism. On the other, it cannot fail to be a temptation to mankind now arrived at the age of reflection, for it concentrates all human life and even religion on man and his anthropocentric perfection. Man cannot submit to the rule of egoism; the earth is not made up only of mountains; religion does not come in order to slay man but to save him. The staggering affirmation of christian belief is just that it is vitally necessary to save not only the 'lofty' part of man, his soul, but the whole man including his body, indeed the whole cosmos. By stressing these truths lopsidedly, however, humanism very easily loses sight of the whole, upsets the balance and tends to become sheer naturalism.

A religion that is simply humanist is a religion of compromise, running the risk of reducing itself merely to moralism and of emptying spirituality of its most specific dimension. All true spirituality, we may say, is centred upon the point of arrival (God), not upon the point of departure (man). It is based upon the existing union between the two poles—created and uncreated —of human existence, and not upon a dualism which would confront and oppose them to one another (for example, the 'couples' [*dvandva*] theology-philosophy, supernatural-natural, sacred-profane, city of God-city of man, good-evil, God-men etc.). Religion is not the opium of the people but no more is it their bread, even though it has sometimes succeeded in proffering bread and though even a little opium may from time to time be salutary when there is no other remedy possible. One cannot reduce religion to mere humanism. One cannot eliminate from the mystery of Christ the dimension of the Father in which it finds its fullness and consummation. Religion is not simply anthropomorphism; Christ is not only the divine child, the 'prisoner of the tabernacle', gentle Jesus, the slave of the whimsies (or theological fantasies) of men. Paradise is not found on earth and the saint is not necessarily the humanly speaking perfect man. Christianity is not any sort of humanism and even the expression 'christian humanism' is a contradiction in terms. One can say as much of any religion or quasi-religion.

If the spiritual attitude of humanism is one-sided and thus dangerous, untrue, moreover, even when it makes itself out to be the one and only true spirituality, the dualism which is its presupposition is a doctrinal error parallel to atheism. The humanist attitude, however, offers unceasing witness to the utmost dignity of human life upon earth and reminds us that personal liberty and the irresistible demand of 'thy will be done' are essential elements of all true spirituality.

ANGELISM

The dangers inherent in the spirituality of the Spirit are the reverse of those which threaten humanism. Man most certainly is not an angel. Why then, to put it briefly, is the assertion still so frequently made that 'man is not pure spirit!' Does not such a remark betray a yearning for the angelism that was so marked a feature of certain periods of history? Since he is not pure spirit, must man then be considered *impure spirit*—impure on account of his body? It is as if to be what he is, namely man, were for him an imperfection, a stigma, even a shame; this is tantamount to saying that man is a fallen angel and that the real goal of his nature is to reach an angelic, i.e. purely spiritual, plane. Now man is not 'pure spirit' nor is he simply 'spirit'. One may call him if one so desires, an 'embodied spirit' but it would be equally correct to call him 'spiritualised body'. The use of the word 'spirituality' to denote the path of man towards perfection betrays similarly a disdain for or forgetfulness of the bodily, although the body and matter are religious elements just as important as the rest. Yet, when the body is not rejected outright, it is most often forgotten or disregarded. Is not the 'discovery' of the concept of soul simply an attempt to save man by freeing him from the weight of his body? The soul becomes then the immortal element destined for salvation, while the rest can with impunity be jettisoned. Why is the *jivan-mukta* considered a realised soul, with no need henceforth of the temporal sphere and no further duty towards society, if not because only the soul, and even more the 'fine point' of the soul, is deemed worthy of man?

It is a fact—and one that is full of significance—that the Church has generally shown herself far more severe towards this type of spiritual movement than towards opposite tendencies erring on the side of laxity. Is not what I here call angelism the selfsame thing that crops up through the centuries under various names and forms within the Church : montanism, quietism, jansenism, esotericism, puritanism, etc? *Corruptio optimi pessimo* —the corruption of the best is the worst of all. Is it not the greatest pitfall of all religions?

In the spirituality of the Spirit there is a fundamental dimension that it is of urgent importance to recapture, for the evolution of the west and the corresponding present-day emphasis in the east upon material values are driving men towards a sharp decline to which throughout history man's nature has been all too prone—towards a loss of interiority and the rejection of the primacy of eschatology. It is at this point that hinduism of a certain kind makes a valuable contribution; by directing our attention again and again to the Absolute, it reminds us powerfully of the reality of the Spirit, bringing to us an understanding in depth of its primordial role in human life and its sublimating work. In this way we come to understand better the basic inconsistency of that which at first sight appears to us to constitute reality.

If the spirituality of the Spirit is not anchored by being integrated in the Trinity it falls into the doctrinal error of *pantheism*. It bears witness, certainly, to our life and our existence *in* God (in him we live and move and have our being) but it has no right to ignore the fact that our life is still *in the making,* that it is *in fieri,* be-coming, that there is within us a movement towards the Absolute and that we have not yet arrived at Being though Being has already come to us.

* * * *

It is now perhaps easier to understand what I wish to indicate by the word *theandrism*; it is a spirituality which combines in an authentic synthesis the three dimensions of our life on earth as well as in heaven. In it are to be found *contemplation* that is something more than thought, *action* which does not limit its purview to the building of an earthly city, *God* who, is not solely a judge or a scrutinising Eye, *love* that surpasses all sentimentality, *prayer* that is not limited to petition or even to praise but also *silence* that does not fall into indifference, *apophatism* that does not get bogged down in nihilism, *super-naturalism* that is not antinatural—in short, a sense of the Spirit that is not disincarnate combined with a sense of Incarnation that does not neglect the Spirit, an *affirmation* that is not exclusive and a *negation* that is not closed in upon itself.

This is a spirituality whose most simple expression would say : Man is more than 'man'; he is a theandric mystery.